MEDIA ABUSES: RIGHTS AND REMEDIES

A Guide to Legal Remedies

The Media Institute is a nonprofit, tax-exempt research foundation supported by a wide range of foundations, corporations, associations and individuals. The Institute has published a number of studies analyzing television evening news coverage of major economic issues. The Institute also sponsors various programs related to business/media relations and communications issues, both domestic and international.

THE MEDIA INSTITUTE
3017 M Street, N.W.
Washington, D.C. 20007
202/298-7512

Media Abuses: Rights and Remedies

A Guide to Legal Remedies

With a Foreword by Leonard J. Theberge

the media institute

Washington, D.C.

MEDIA ABUSES: RIGHTS AND REMEDIES
A Guide to Legal Remedies

First printing October 1983.

Published by The Media Institute, Washington, D.C.

Printed in the United States of America.

ISBN: 0-937790-20-6

Library of Congress Catalog Card Number: 83-062176

TABLE OF CONTENTS

ACKNOWLEDGMENTS

The Media Institute wishes to thank the many persons who helped prepare this volume since the idea for a reference book on administrative and judicial remedies was conceived some years ago.

This edition began as a report prepared by Leon T. Knauer, Esq. and Stephen A. Hildebrandt, Esq. of Wilkinson, Cragun & Barker (Washington, D.C.) for the Southeastern and Capital Legal Foundations. Rosel H. Hyde, Esq., and Kenneth D. Patrich and Kenneth E. Satten, law clerks, contributed substantial assistance, research and substantive suggestions.

Subsequently, the report was expanded and updated for The Media Institute by Dianne Hubbard, a Harvard law student, and Timothy G. Brown, Esq., a member of the Ontario Bar. Mr. Brown is largely responsible for the book's final form. Mary Powers typed the final text, which was edited by Richard T. Kaplar and James W. Quiggle of the Institute.

FOREWORD

In the past, Media Institute studies have concentrated on evaluating the content of television coverage. These analyses have often identified serious distortions in the media's presentation of vital public issues. The Institute has been successful in documenting deficiencies in media coverage, but it has not, until now, addressed the larger question of how to correct them.

This study represents an important step in this direction. For the first time, the Institute presents an analysis dealing with the administrative and judicial remedies available to victims of distorted media coverage. The significance of this type of study is clear. In American society, the media continue to play a major role in shaping public discussion and opinion. It is important that citizens be aware of the remedies available to them when the media's treatment of public issues becomes distorted or unbalanced.

However, even the briefest examination of this study reveals that remedies for media distortion are not especially numerous or effective. Both administrative and judicial solutions suffer from serious limitations. For those aggrieved, the efficacy of either approach depends on their overall objectives and the circumstances surrounding the distorted coverage.

The study points out that administrative remedies, which come under the jurisdiction of the Federal Communications Commission (FCC), may be effective for those seeking a more balanced presentation of public issues. The FCC cannot, however, award monetary damages to individuals or business entities wronged by prior excesses of the media. In addition, the FCC allows broad discretion to broadcasters in their presentation of public issues and has little interest in investigating charges of deliberate distortion in media coverage. While administrative remedies are easier to implement, they lack the teeth necessary to deter serious media misconduct.

Judicial remedies afford the possibility of monetary damages for media distortions, but often place a heavy burden of proof on the aggrieved parties. For persons or groups in the public arena, proof of mere negligence by the media is insufficient to obtain compensation from the guilty party. "Public figures" damaged by distorted coverage have the difficult and most often impossible task of proving "actual malice."

The Institute's study is a careful examination of the options available to aggrieved parties. The low success rate it reports raises some important policy questions.

The enormous discretion allowed broadcasters in determining what issues warrant balanced coverage raises the danger that new ideas or viewpoints will have difficulty in obtaining an adequate public forum. The Institute's study reveals one FCC decision that national defense was not an issue requiring balanced presentation because it was "of insufficient specificity." If the conventional wisdom determines what constitutes a valid issue, then the deck is already stacked against individuals who offer an alternative perspective on major social questions.

Another point raised by the Institute's study is the degree to which corporations and individuals are viewed as public entities. The tendency of the courts to broadly define the public realm places a heavy burden on those seeking to reduce the harm done to them by media misconduct. It appears that a desire for unhampered public discussion has led the courts to blur valid and necessary distinctions between public and private activity.

Finally, there is the question of a reporter's privilege not to disclose news sources. For years, reporters have refused to reveal information related to their news gathering -- claiming protection under the First Amendment. In many instances this refusal has hampered non-media parties to court proceedings in obtaining information vital to their case.

In recent years, the courts have limited newsmen's right to withhold sources. Many state legislatures, however, have clouded the issue by enacting shield laws which maintain the reporter's privileged position. The situation varies widely from state to state and it is still unclear how the First Amendment rights of the press will ultimately be reconciled with the right of individuals to a fair trial.

Media Abuses: Rights and Remedies is a practical guide for those who wish to determine if media coverage has violated their rights. The limited success of such efforts, however, points to the need for a continuing public discussion of the media's role in society. It is vital that we maintain a system of information dissemination that is free from government interference. At the same time we must not allow that freedom to squelch diverse views, to damage the reputations and livelihoods of private citizens, to deny privacy or to prevent a defendant from securing a fair trial. The Media Institute's study indicates that an examination of the balance between these competing social objectives is essential to the well-being of our democracy.

Leonard J. Theberge
President
The Media Institute

INTRODUCTION

This report outlines the remedies available when a radio or television station broadcast is biased, distorted or untrue, and injures the reputation of a citizen, commercial entity or its principals.

The remedies discussed are those (1) before the Federal Communications Commission, which has regulatory jurisdiction over radio and television stations, and (2) before the courts, whose jurisdiction would be based on tort or negligence principles. The discussion on judicial relief includes a commentary on the rights and limitations of the media when gathering news. Both administrative and judicial remedies may be pursued. They are not exclusive.

The administrative remedies before the Federal Communications Commission have the benefits of being inexpensive and relatively simple to compile. The detriments are that there is no right to discovery; the burden of proof is almost exclusively on the complainant; substantial time elapses before a decision is rendered; and the remedies are generally inadequate.

The benefits of seeking judicial relief are that a commercial entity can frequently select a court in the most favorable jurisdiction; discovery of the media is permitted; and damages may be awarded. Also, recent court decisions have relaxed the heretofore strict standards which severely restricted efforts to sue the electronic media for false or libelous comments. The detriments are that court litigation is expensive and time-consuming, and the plaintiff is seldom successful.

On the following page is a summary chart comparing the benefits of administrative and judicial remedies.

SUMMARY OF COMPARATIVE BENEFITS: ADMINISTRATIVE vs. JUDICIAL REMEDIES*

BENEFITS	ADMINISTRATIVE	JUDICIAL
Substantive Choice of favorable jurisdiction		X
Liability for stations and individuals		X
Pursue complaint not solely in public interest		X
Remedy for broadcast of false information		X
Remedy for broadcast of true information	X	X
Remedy for broadcast of opinions/comment	X	
Lower standard of proof for public figures	X	
Lower standard of proof for private individuals	X	
No need to prove fault	X	
Procedural Simplicity	X	
Speed	X	
Expense (amount)	X	
Expenses (recovery by winner)		X
Remedies Possible Air time for reply	X	
Affect broadcast license	X	
Broadcaster subject to monetary fines	X	
Money awarded for injury		X
Punitive damages		X

*Some, none or all of these benefits will be enjoyed depending on: (1) nature of the offending broadcast, (2) type of injury suffered, (3) nature of relief sought, (4) the specific remedy sought, (5) public or private status of complainant, and (6) law applicable in jurisdiction where remedy pursued.

ADMINISTRATIVE RELIEF

I. Fairness Doctrine

The Fairness Doctrine imposes on broadcasters the obligation to give a "fair break" to all responsible positions on a controversial issue of public importance. The station decides how to meet this obligation; the proponents of any given responsible position do not have the right to select a spokesman; and the station can rely on material broadcast before and after the disputed program to defend its claim that all responsible positions were given a "fair break."

A. General Principles

1. Broadcasting and Free Speech Under the Constitution and the Communications Act, free speech does not include the unqualified right of a broadcaster[1] to espouse a particular view. Rather, an affirmative obligation has been imposed on the broadcaster to maintain and enhance a system of free expression by assuring the widest possible dissemination of information from diverse and antagonistic sources. This obligation is known as the Fairness Doctrine and requires a broadcaster to:

(i) Devote a reasonable amount of program time to the discussion of public issues, and

(ii) Devote a reasonable amount of program time to the dissemination of opposing or differing viewpoints.

The Fairness Doctrine obligation differentiates the broadcast media from the print media by restricting broadcasters' First Amendment freedom to program and editorialize. This restriction is based on the theory of spectrum scarcity. Because radio and TV spectrum space is limited, the Commission requires affirmative action designed to enhance free speech. The Supreme Court has upheld the constitutionality of the Fairness Doctrine, stating that the differences between the broadcast media and the print media justify differences in the applicability of First Amendment standards.[2] In sum, the television medium has less First Amendment protection than the print medium and is subject to more federal regulation. Monitoring compliance with these regulations, and demanding compliance when a violation is suspected, can be helpful to parties who feel they have been unfairly treated by the TV broadcast medium.

2. Specifics of the Fairness Doctrine Television broadcasters must select issues, spokesmen, amounts of time and formats that assure controversial issues are properly addressed. The role of the Federal Communications Commission is simply to rule on the reasonableness of broadcasters' judgments, not to second-guess them.

A TV broadcaster does not have to address every controversial issue. However, in the Commission's view, some controversial issues are so important that to ignore them would be unreasonable.

The obligation to cover controversial issues of public importance is seldom enforced. The only recent instance where it was invoked was the 1976 Patsy Mink case.[3] A West Virginia television station was found in violation of the Fairness Doctrine for failing to air any programming on pending strip-mining legislation -- a highly controversial issue with tremendous local impact.

In deciding what qualifies as a controversial issue of public importance, broadcasters are required to consider the degree of attention paid to the particular issue by the media, the government and responsible community leaders. The standard is whether the matter is "the subject of vigorous debate with substantial elements of the community in opposition to each other." Any measure on which voters are asked to vote is, by definition, a controversial issue of public importance.

Once an issue has been mentioned, the television broadcaster is held to the standard of "good faith" in deciding whether to present opposing viewpoints and, if so, the amount of time to be allocated. Factors such as time of day, frequency of broadcast and the nature of the audience must be considered. There is no mathematical formula for measuring these factors; in each instance, the FCC determines whether the broadcaster has acted "reasonably."

In resolving Fairness Doctrine complaints, the Commission takes a case-by-case approach, rather than waiting until the station applies to renew its license. The Commission believes it can best determine whether a station has been "fair" by examining the programs related to a specific topic, instead of evaluating all the programming on all subjects at license renewal time.

A person with a Fairness Doctrine complaint must first contact the station and request relief. Barring unusual circumstances, complaints will not be considered by the Commission unless the broadcaster has been afforded an opportunity to comply with the complainant's request or to explain its position.[4]

3. Facts Which Must Be Asserted. A complaint must present *prima facie* evidence of a violation of the Fairness Doctrine. The initial burden is squarely on the complaining party.[5] The complaint, a copy of which should be sent to the station, should contain the following:

(i) The name of the station or network involved;

(ii) The specific controversial issue of public importance which was addressed;

(iii) The dates and times of the broadcasts;

(iv) The reasons why the issue is both controversial and of public importance;

(v) An accurate summary of the view broadcast;

(vi) The basis of the claim that the station or network has not broadcast contrasting views on the issue in its overall programming; and

(vii) Whether the station or network has afforded, or has expressed the intention to afford, a reasonable opportunity for the presentation of contrasting views on the issue.[6]

A complainant must demonstrate a lack of contrasting viewpoints because a station can meet its Fairness Doctrine obligations in its overall programming -- a station does not have to offer a forum for differing views in the same program or series of programs. In the past, *prima facie* claims of the absence of a conflicting viewpoint have been based on the personal knowledge of a complainant, who recited that as a matter of routine, he followed the news, public affairs and other non-entertainment programming carried by the station involved.[7]

However, the Commission has indicated that future claims will not be so easily established, and as a complaint progresses the burden of proof on a complainant becomes very heavy indeed. Most complaints fail because the complainant cannot prove a lack of balanced programming, and the broadcaster can refuse to reveal the programming information needed as proof.

B. Application of Fairness Doctrine to Commercial Advertisements

The Fairness Doctrine applies to commercial advertisements if they include a direct and significant commentary on important public issues. There must, however, be a substantial relationship between the commercial and an ongoing public debate.[8]

For example, the Fairness Doctrine was applied to cigarette advertisements until 1967 (when broadcasters were prohibited from carrying any cigarette commercials). The Commission has since held that cigarette advertisements were unique, and the Fairness Doctrine would probably not be applied to other ads that merely offer commercial products for sale.[9] The Fairness Doctrine could apply, however, to commercial advertisements relating to such things as oil, nuclear power, forest usage and pesticides, if the ads advocate positions on the controversial issues of pollution, public safety, conservation or public health. In recent years, special-interest groups, who avowedly represent segments of the public, have demanded the right to counterbalance advertisements of business entities such as petroleum and utility companies. These groups have generally been unsuccessful except where a referendum was being presented to the voters on an issue like nuclear power.[10]

A few recent cases will illustrate the Commission's approach to Fairness Doctrine complaints about corporate advertisements. In 1976, a Washington, D.C., television station was found in violation of the Doctrine for airing a series of advertisements about mandatory divestiture by major oil companies. The advertisements implied that vertically integrated oil companies were the best means of efficiently exploiting energy resources. The advertisements, which had been aired 53 times over a period of three and a half months, did not specifically mention divestiture, but did show the pieces of a puzzle, each representing one particular phase of the oil business, and referred to those pieces coming together. The Commission ruled that the station, which took the position that this was not a controversial issue of public importance, would have to present more programming in support of oil company divestiture to fulfill its Fairness Doctrine obligations.[11] Explicit "editorial" advertisements are likely to fall under the Fairness Doctrine.

In 1979, the Commission found 12 radio stations in violation of the Doctrine for failing to balance a series of advertisements praising nuclear power.[12] But, by way of contrast, in 1982, the Commission declared that another series of commercials advocating nuclear power plant construction did not trigger the Fairness Doctrine. The complainants asserted that these ads presented one side of the issue of how future energy needs should be met. The station argued that the commercials simply stated an undisputed fact -- that solar energy is not a sufficient source of energy for the near future. The Commission ruled that the issue, however stated, was not currently controversial, and that the complainant had not presented sufficient evidence of an imbalance in overall programming.[13]

Broadcasters often cite the Fairness Doctrine as a rationale for refusing certain types of corporate advertising, but "image spots" that project a favorable public image of a corporation have generally been found not to make statements triggering the Doctrine.[14] And recently the courts have held that a complete ban on "paid public issue announcements" (such as statements against nuclear power or the use of pesticides) would violate the First Amendment if other types of paid announcements are accepted by broadcast stations.[15] However, the courts have refrained from requiring broadcasters to afford time to any particular group or citizen. It should be noted that most Fairness Doctrine complaints about paid advertisements are denied by the Commission.

C. Fairness Doctrine Matters Which Should Be Considered by Business Entities

1. Defining the "Issue" A business entity confronted with a potential Fairness Doctrine problem must first determine whether the subject matter of the broadcast is both controversial and of public importance. This determination could apply to a commercial advertisement being considered by the business entity; the commercial advertisement of a competitor; or any other program broadcasting opinions on issues relevant to the entity's business.

Identifying the issue is perhaps the most difficult aspect of the Fairness Doctrine. Many of the cases dismissed by the Commission are disqualified on the grounds that no controversial issue of public importance has been raised. This result often stems from differing interpretations of the issue at hand. For example, the documentary "Pensions: The Broken Promise" focused on abuses of private pension plans. The complainant argued that the program was a one-sided look at private pension plans in general. The broadcaster countered that the show only dealt with problems in some private pension plans. The Commission agreed with the complainant, but the decision was reversed by a court of appeals.[16]

Historically, the Commission has required the airing of opposing viewpoints on such issues as nuclear power[17] and the Alaskan pipeline.[18] In 1979 the courts overturned a Commission decision that national defense and national security were of insufficient specificity to be Fairness Doctrine issues.[19] However, from a statistical standpoint, very few Fairness Doctrine complaints are successful.

2. Time Factors Inordinate time normally elapses before a Fairness Doctrine complaint is resolved -- more than a year, on average, and frequently longer. For example, in October 1974, the American Security Council Educational Foundation complained to CBS about distorted news presentations on national defense. On September 8, 1976, after CBS had denied any violation of the Fairness Doctrine, the Foundation filed a Fairness Doctrine complaint against the network. On March 15, 1977, the Federal Communications Commission found that "no Commission action was warranted."[20] The Foundation appealed. On September 13, 1978, the Court sent the case back to the Commission with instructions to investigate the practices of CBS in reporting on national defense.[21] However, that decision was vacated in June 1979. Finally, almost five years after the action was initiated, the FCC's dismissal of the complaint was left standing.

3. Limited Remedies The remedies of a Fairness Doctrine complaint are often of limited value. Even in the case of a favorable ruling, the amount of time elapsed since the initial broadcast may render the response ineffective. Furthermore, the station has discretion to select the spokesman, the time and the format for the presentation of opposing viewpoints, and it might very well elect to ignore the original complainant in complying with the Fairness Doctrine.

4. Complaint Must Be In Public Interest Finally, a Fairness Doctrine complaint instituted by a business entity may be subject to closer scrutiny than complaints from other sources. The business entity normally must show that the issue involved is one of public interest (as opposed to corporate interest). The Commission has rejected complaints because, it held, pecuniary interest was the motivating factor behind the complaint of a business entity.[22] That is, the Commission appeared to reject the complaint because the only possible injury was to the complainant's business.

5. Costs One important consideration is attorneys' fees or costs. In an FCC fight these costs are not reimbursed -- not even to the winning party. And lawyers' fees in a Fairness Doctrine case can be substantial, almost as much as in a full-blown lawsuit.

D. Conclusion

A business entity should understand the serious limitations of the Fairness Doctrine complaint procedure before deciding to pursue this remedy at the Commission. The chances of success are minimal; the effort is time-consuming; and the result is often ineffective. On the other hand, most stations do take their Fairness Doctrine responsibilities seriously. Therefore, a well-documented complaint to the station, with a copy to the Commission, may engender a favorable station response without any formal action by the Commission. If the complaint is filed around the time when the station's license renewal is being considered by the Commission, the station might prefer to satisfy the complainant rather than possibly delay its license renewal through a protracted Fairness Doctrine fight. (This is unlikely, however, because the Commission has a stated policy that unresolved Fairness Doctrine complaints will not delay license renewals.) If the station does decide to fight the complaint tenaciously, all the limitations noted above come into play and other avenues of redress probably would be more effective. The issue may become moot if proposals to eliminate the Fairness Doctrine, now pending in Congress, are passed.[23] The current Commission membership favors deregulation.[24]

II. Personal Attack Rules

When the honesty, character, integrity or like personal qualities of a person or other entity have been assailed in a broadcast on a controversial issue of public importance, the station must give the person or other entity assailed the transcript and afford comparable time to respond, regardless of the truth of the broadcast.

A. General Application

The personal attack rules (considered part of the Fairness Doctrine) impose very specific requirements on broadcasters. Of special interest to a business entity is the guarantee of reply time on the station.

A personal attack is defined as a statement made against the "honesty, character, integrity or like personal qualities of an identified person or a group." The attack must be made during the presentation of views on a controversial issue of public importance.

The Commission's rules do not prohibit the broadcast of such attacks; however, a station must do the following within one week after the attack is broadcast:

(i) Notify the person or group attacked of the date, time and title of the program on which the attack was made;

(ii) Send the person or group attacked a script or tape of the attack, or an accurate summary if neither of these is available; and

(iii) Offer the person attacked a "reasonable opportunity" to answer the attack over the air.[25]

Unlike libel laws where the truth is always a defense, the truth or falsity of a personal attack is irrelevant to the personal attack rules. The station must comply with the rules and offer reply time to a person who was attacked, even if the attack was clearly true.

These rules provide an effective and immediate method for challenging statements broadcast about the honesty, character or integrity of a private citizen, corporation or corporate officer. The station is absolutely required to give the party attacked an opportunity to respond at a time of day and for an amount of time comparable to those in which the attack was broadcast. If the station refuses or neglects its responsibility under this rule, and the Commission becomes aware of it through complaint or otherwise, it can impose a substantial fine on the station. Repeated violation of the rule can be grounds for revocation of the station's license.

B. Exceptions

There are two major exceptions to the personal attack rules.

First, the rules do not apply to personal attacks made by legally qualified political candidates, or their authorized spokesmen, against other candidates or their authorized spokesmen. Thus, most political broadcasts will not raise personal attack issues. However, if a candidate attacks a corporation, corporate officer, or other individual, who is not a candidate (or associated with a candidate), the personal attack rules do apply.

Second, personal attacks made in a bona fide newscast, a bona fide news interview, or on-the-spot coverage of a bona fide news event are excluded from the personal attack rules. However, news documentaries and editorials carried in newscasts are not exempted, and attacks made during these broadcasts would trigger the personal attack rules.

C. Examples

Several Commission decisions illustrate what the Commission considers a personal attack on the honesty, character, integrity or like personal quality of a person or a group.

In one case, a station accused county supervisors of "strange mental gymnastics" in voting for a bond issue to enlarge the county government's office space.[26] The Commission rejected the complaint and held that the station had not been unreasonable in deciding that no personal attack had been made, "because the editorial questioned the wisdom of the supervisors' positions and not their honesty, character or integrity."

In another case, a woman was referred to as "the garrulous grand dame of Billings radio talk show" and a "pistol-packing mama."[27] The Commission refused to find against the station because "The statements [did] not appear to allege either a deliberate falsehood or to question the character or integrity of the person."

In a third case, a station broadcast charges that a local leader's "veracity leaves something to be desired" and that his "constituents had best assess his integrity or lack of it."[28] The Commission imposed a fine on the licensee for violation of the personal attack rule because the veracity and integrity of the person had been questioned.

D. Defenses

The most common defenses which stations raise when accused of broadcasting personal attacks are:

(i) The attack was not made upon the honesty, character, integrity or like personal quality of the person or group;

(ii) The attack was not made on an "identified" person or group, but rather was a general criticism;

(iii) The attack was made during a bona fide newscast, news interview, or on-the-spot coverage of a bona fide news event; and

(iv) The attack was not made during a discussion of a controversial issue of public importance.

Each of these is a valid defense as long as there are supportive facts.

E. Applicability of Rules to Business Entities

If a broadcast attacks the honesty, character, integrity or like personal quality of an identified person (such as a corporate officer or director), or an identified group (such as a corporation or its board of directors), there is an absolute responsibility to notify the entity attacked, provide a transcript and offer a reasonable opportunity to respond over the air. In case of a personal atack, a complainant should first inform the station that a personal attack has taken place, and demand a script or tape of the attack, plus reply time. If broadcast time is denied, or the information is not provided within one week of the attack, a complaint may be addressed to the Commission.

Two cases involving alleged personal attacks against business entities illustrate how the Commission often handles such complaints and the potential hurdles which a business complainant must overcome to obtain remedial action from the Commission.

In one case it was alleged that a station's talk show host spent 20 minutes attacking a company.[29] The host claimed that the company had "lied to the Michigan Public Service Commission," had "claimed phantom taxes," had paid "excessive salaries," had "incompetent management," and had "a license to steal." The Commission denied relief in this case on two grounds: (i) the complainant had been offered an opportunity to reply on several of the station's programs; and (ii) the complainant had not provided information to the Commission that the attack took place during the discussion of a controversial issue of public importance.

This case illustrates several factors which are important to consider if a business entity decides to bring a personal attack complaint. First, the burden of proof is on the business entity complainant. Second, even if an attack is made on the honesty, character, integrity or like personal quality of the business or its officers, such an attack will not constitute a violation of the Commission's personal attack rules unless it is made during a discussion of a controversial issue of public importance. In this case there was no showing that a controversial issue of public importance had been under discussion, and therefore, the Commission could make no ruling on whether the personal attack rules had been violated. Finally, a complainant must accept a reasonable offer of opportunities to respond, even if he does not particularly like the format offered by the station. For example, if the station offers an opportunity to respond on the same talk show on which the attack was made, the business cannot claim that such a forum is inherently unfair, and should not reject the opportunity. Rather, the business must accept the opportunity and afterward complain to the FCC that such a forum was inherently unfair (if it still believes the opportunity to respond was inadequate).

A personal attack of a "passing nature," which is not germane to the subject matter under discussion, will not trigger the personal attack rules and will warrant no Commission action. In a 1977 program relating to the disclosure of classified documents by government employees, CBS mentioned that the Lockheed Corp. had "robbed the taxpayers blind" in connection with its contract for the production of the C5-A aircraft. The Commission ruled that the broadcast was devoted entirely to a discussion of an executive order about disclosure of classified information by government employees, and the show did not, in any substantial manner, deal with the Lockheed C5-A contract.[30] The attack on Lockheed was ruled incidental and peripheral to the subject under discussion, and, accordingly, did not meet the requirements of the Commission's personal attack rule. Of course, such attacks may still provide grounds for court actions on the basis of libel or slander.

III. Political Broadcasting

Candidates for public office are statutorily entitled to "equal opportunity" once a station has permitted an opposing candidate to use its facilities or has editorialized on behalf of the opposing candidate. Broadcasters must also provide "reasonable access" to candidates for federal elective office. Generally, the Fairness Doctrine and the Personal Attack rules do not apply to broadcasts by candidates for public office.

A. General Regulations

The Congress and the Commission established specific laws, rules and policies regarding broadcasts by political candidates and their supporters. The Fairness Doctrine and the Personal Attack rules do not normally apply to broadcasts by candidates for public office. The basic law of political broadcasting is contained in sections 315 and 312(a)(c) of the Communications Act of 1934, as amended. They can generally be summarized as requiring "equal opportunities" and "reasonable access" for political candidates.

The political broadcasting laws and rules apply only to programs or announcements in which candidates take part personally, either by voice or picture. They apply regardless of what the candidate talks about, and any kind of an appearance counts as a "use" of the station under these laws. For example, if an actor or comedian is a candidate for public office, his appearance in a motion picture, drama or comedy on a station would entitle his political opponents to equal opportunities on that station, even if no mention of his candidacy was made during the program.[31]

Determining whether someone is a legally qualified candidate is complicated under the rules and has been interpreted by many cases. In general, however, the candidate must be eligible under the law to hold the office, announce that he is a candidate for nomination or election, and must qualify for a place on the ballot or publicly commit himself to seeking election as a write-in candidate.

Stations must retain public records of all requests for time made by, or on behalf of, political candidates and the outcome of each request, i.e., whether air time was provided or not, when it was provided, and what rates, if any, were chargea by the station. Gifts of time to candidates, whether requested or not, also must be recorded in the public files.

1. Equal Opportunities If a broadcaster permits a legally qualified candidate for any public office to go on the air, "equal opportunities" must be afforded all other such candidates for that office. Advertising rates charged all legally qualified candidates must be the lowest unit rate of the station for the same class and amount of time.

But equal opportunities does not mean "equal time." The phrase "equal time" is never used in the law. Equal opportunities usually includes equal time, but the term means much more. For example, it includes the right to obtain time in a period likely to attract approximately the same size audience as the period in which the opposing candidate appeared.

A candidate who desires equal opportunity must make his request within one week of the day on which his opponent made his broadcast. Therefore, if one candidate has been appearing on a station for five weeks and his opponent does not request equal opportunities until the end of the fifth week, the opponent would probably be entitled only to the amount of time that the candidate had used during the fifth week.

Equal opportunities for opposing candidates need not be provided by a broadcaster if the appearance by a candidate is on a bona fide newscast, news interview, news documentary, or on-the-spot coverage of news events.

2. Reasonable Access "Reasonable access" means that a broadcaster must allow legally qualified candidates for federal elective office to have reasonable amounts of time on the station.[32] It should be noted that the station cannot censor any material broadcast by political candidates.

The Commission has a number of rules and policies concerning what constitutes "reasonable access" for a federal candidate. Some of the more important principles include the following:

(i) Generally, broadcast stations must make "prime time" program time available. This means program time in the evening hours on television and during drive time on radio;

(ii) Commercial stations must always make "prime time" commercial announcements available;

(iii) Generally, stations must make the same type and class of time available to federal candidates which they normally make available to commercial advertisers;

(iv) The reasonable access requirement applies to time periods 45 days before a primary election and 60 days before a general election;

(v) Non-commercial educational stations have the same obligations as commercial stations; and

(vi) A candidate need not be given or sold any particular position on the station's schedule.[33]

3. Political Editorials Another rule relating to political broadcasting is the Commission's policy on political editorials.[34] Political editorials are statements in which the station itself endorses or opposes a particular candidate. The rules do not forbid broadcasting political editorials. They do, however, require that a broadcaster send to all candidates for the same office the following information, within 24 hours after the editorial:

(i) Notification of the date and time of the editorial;

(ii) A script or tape of the editorial; and

(iii) An offer of an opportunity for the candidate or a spokesman to respond over the air.

In conclusion, federal law and the rules of the Commission provide a detailed set of obligations in the political arena. These rules are designed to make sure the candidates are allowed to speak freely on the air without censorship and to prevent discrimination among competing candidates by broadcasters.

B. Referenda and the Fairness Doctrine

Any issue which will be subject to a vote is, by definition, a controversial issue of public importance giving rise to Fairness Doctrine obligations.[35]

A recent Supreme Court case has confirmed the right of corporations to speak out on all referendum issues.[36] The Court struck down a Massachusetts statute which prohibited corporations from commenting on ballot questions unless the question materially affected the corporation's business. The Court stated that there could be no distinction between corporations and other groups in protecting their First Amendment freedom of speech and their right to comment on referenda submitted to a public vote. The Court stated:

> If the speakers here were not corporations, no one would suggest that the State could silence their proposed speech. It is the type of speech indispensible to decision-making in a democracy, and this is no less true because the speech comes from a corporation rather than an individual. The inherent worth of the speech in terms of its capacity for informing the public does not depend upon the identity of its source, whether corporation, association, union or individual.[37]

Corporations, therefore, may purchase time on radio and television to comment on ballot initiatives which are of interest to them. But such broadcasts will impose Fairness Doctrine obligations on stations that air them.

Consider the Commission's handling of complaints about California ballot initiatives on nuclear power. In this case,[38] corporations ran commercial advertisements extolling the virtues of nuclear power, at the same time that nuclear power was a referendum issue. Fairness Doctrine complaints were brought against the stations running these advertisements. The Commission held that because of the ballot initiative, nuclear power was indeed a controversial issue of public importance in California, and that advertisements directly espousing the pro-nuclear position triggered the Fairness Doctrine. The Commission required the stations to balance their programming by running, prior to the vote, anti-nuclear power ads of comparable frequency, and in comparable time periods. Frequency ratios of 5:1 have been judged "comparable" by the Commission. This is not an equal-time concept.

Thus, the broadcast by a radio or television station of a particular view on a ballot issue does not trigger the specific "equal opportunities" or "political editorial" rules discussed above. Rather, the broadcast of a particular view on a ballot initiative is governed by the general provisions of the Fairness Doctrine. Therefore, a station would be required to generally balance its programming on both sides of the ballot initiative issue prior to election day, and may have to give away free time to achieve that balance. For this reason, some stations, like KNXT in Los Angeles, restrict the time they will sell to "issue" advertisers. CBS and NBC refuse to accept issue ads and ABC will only broadcast them after 11:30 p.m. Corporations are legally allowed to buy air time to speak out on public issues, but no broadcaster can be compelled to sell air time for that purpose.

IV. News Distortion

News distortion or news staging is the intentional misrepresentation of news events, and it is unlikely that the Commission will take any remedial action against a station unless there is solid, extrinsic evidence of deliberate distortion or staging.

The Commission will not investigate charges of misrepresentation of news in the absence of extrinsic evidence which shows on its face, deliberate distortion by a broadcaster. As an example of extrinsic evidence, the Commission has cited "testimony in writing or otherwise from 'insiders' or persons who have direct personal knowledge of an intentional attempt to falsify the news."[39]

Although the Commission has concluded that "rigging or slanting news is a most heinous act against the public interest," complaints of deliberate distortion will have no effect on license renewals unless the charges involve top management.

Clear evidence of news rigging, such as outtakes or memoranda, or extrinsic evidence that a newsman had been given a bribe (or had offered a bribe to procure some action or statement), would normally warrant a Commission investigation. Usually, however, the Commission merely refers the matter to the station for its own investigations, or takes no action at all on news distortion complaints.

Of special interest is the situation where a person quoted on a news program complains that he clearly said something else. In these cases, the Commission does not feel that it can "appropriately enter the quagmire of investigating the credibility of the newsman and the interviewed party."[40] These matters are typically referred to the broadcaster for his own investigation, or are dismissed.

One Commission decision in this area illustrates the hard line the Commission adopts in routinely dismissing news distortion complaints. The Black Producers Association complained that ABC had deliberately "staged" certain fight scenes in the news documentary "Youth Terror: The View From Behind the Gun." A statement from a member of the program's production staff, and audio tape recordings of interviews with four persons shown in the program were submitted as evidence. The Commission concluded that there was conflicting evidence as to staging and, in any event, the scenes could not have been considered significant since they constituted only 38 seconds of a 48-minute program.[41]

However, when a radio station staged a fake kidnapping of one of its employees, the Commission did withdraw the station's license.[42]

As a practical matter, the Commission wants to avoid the responsibility of news authentication. It does not see itself as an "arbiter of truth." In keeping with this philosophy, the Commission normally does not mete out penalties in these cases.

JUDICIAL RELIEF

The Federal Communications Commission has the power to revoke or refuse renewal of broadcast licenses, and to impose fines for station misconduct. But the Commission does not have the right to award damages or adjudicate disputes among private parties. Remedies such as these must be handled by the courts.

Thus, a private citizen or a business entity wronged by a broadcast only can seek from the Federal Communications Commission time on the station to remedy the wrong and, perhaps, gain some satisfaction should the Commission fine the station or impose some sanction on its license. The remedies before the Commission are all too frequently inadequate.

An alternative would be to seek relief in the courts. Even if a person or business entity can establish that monetary damages were suffered as a result of a particular broadcast, the Commission cannot award damages. But courts have that power. Thus, the unique jurisdiction of the courts would be established and the broadcaster could not assert that a remedy should have first been sought before the Commission (the so-called "exhaustion of administrative remedies" rule).

The wronged person or business entity can frequently select a court in the most favorable jurisdiction, because networks do business in many states through their affiliates. In certain states, the law in this area is much more favorable to a business entity complaining about disparaging comments aired by a station.[43]

Moreover, court litigation has the added benefit of the right to discovery, including the right to take the testimony under oath from the station management and the announcer who broadcast the disparaging remarks. Because of the requirement that a broadcaster defend his actions under oath, the possibility of monetary damages and the danger of adverse publicity for the station, using the courts may be a more effective means of assuring fairness and objectivity in broadcasting than relying on the power and policies of the Federal Communications Commission.

Libel Law and the Media

One general principle stands out above all the others in this area: It is difficult to win a libel suit against the media. It can be done, but the track to success is filled with legal potholes, hurdles and the broken remains of earlier failed lawsuits, which can be difficult to get around.

Traditional defamation had two forms -- slander (verbal defamation) and libel (written defamation). But the new technologies have resulted in a blurring of the legal distinctions. Broadcast defamation in modern law is considered a part of libel.

Because of the First Amendment, the media have a constitutional status in libel law. However, the media are not immune from liability. The Constitution is not just the First Amendment with all other principles subservient to it, as many media people appear to believe. Individuals and companies covered by the media have constitutional rights as well. But the courts have generally balanced conflicting constitutional rights with their thumbs on the media side of the scales.

In any lawsuit for libel, the plaintiff has to prove identification (that people would know he was the subject of the libel, whether or not he was referred to by name), publication (that some third party had seen the libelous statement), and that the statement somehow brought him into disrepute.

Under modern libel law, a person suing a member of the media must also prove that the media defendant was at fault to some degree. Generally, private individuals must only prove negligence on the media's part. But public officials and public figures must prove "actual malice" (*i.e.*, that the defendant knew the statement was *false* or that he acted in reckless disregard of its truth or falsity). Libel suits are often lost because a "public" plaintiff can't prove actual malice.

Predicting whether a particular libel victim will be labelled a public official or public figure is an uncertain business. In one case, a high school chemistry teacher was declared a public official, but in another case a high school history teacher was not. The celebrity wife of a prominent industrialist was declared not to be a public figure when her spectacular divorce was reported in the media, but the children of Julius and Ethel Rosenberg were labelled public figures for libel purposes.

The burden of proving actual malice is frequently impossible to meet. And the stakes are high, because libel suits are expensive.

Access to reporters' notes or names of media sources is often necessary to prove libel. Broadcasting and print people alike have frequently been able to keep this kind of information secret by claiming a privilege against disclosure, based on the First Amendment. And a majority of states have passed laws which specifically allow the media to refuse information subpoenaed for use in court. By hiding behind these so-called "shield laws" and claiming constitutional privilege, the media successfully defend against many libel suits.

This muddle is compounded by the fact that each state has developed its own libel law, subject to constitutional restrictions laid down by the Supreme Court. Because the chances of winning vary tremendously from state to state, a critical first step in bringing a libel action is deciding in what court and in what state to sue.

A detailed discussion of some of the intricacies of libel law follows.

I. Defamation

Defamation is a false oral or written statement which injures the character, fame or reputation of a person or other entity. The media generally enjoy a high degree of protection against defamation actions because of the First Amendment guarantee of freedom of speech and press. However, the courts in various states have eroded this protection somewhat.

A. General Principles of Libel

Libel (written defamation) includes broadcast defamation because the wide dissemination of the defamatory broadcast is considered as injurious as printed defamation. Generally, defamation consists of a false statement which tends to expose the subject to hatred, contempt or ridicule; or which tends to diminish the esteem, respect, goodwill or confidence of the subject. It is well-settled that a corporation can be defamed. It is the purpose of this section to clarify the state of defamation law as it relates to business entities, and to provide some insight into options available when defamation occurs.

1. Identification To establish grounds for a libel suit, the object of defamation must be specifically and clearly defined. A libel complaint brought by a souvenir shop was dismissed because a critical news commentary showed only shots of the interior of the shop and did not identify it sufficiently enough to be injurious.[44] Similarly, a case filed by a sportsmen's association whose members felt that they had been maligned by a television documentary on hunting was dismissed because no person was particularly mentioned on the program.[45] A $20 billion libel suit was filed on behalf of "all members of the Islamic faith" against the Public Broadcasting Service for showing the controversial documentary "Death of a Princess." The suit was dismissed as frivolous and without merit.[46] A television station that used photographs of a real estate firm's billboard advertisements to accompany its news report on "blockbusting" real estate tactics could not be sued for libel because the firm was neither named nor explicitly charged with unethical or unlawful business practices.[47]

2. False Statement A statement of fact can be grounds for libel only if it is false. One court ruled that the omission of one statement in a substantially true report does not make it libel.[48] However, another court commented that even if each fact in an article

standing alone is true, "The proper question is whether the meaning reasonably conveyed by the published words is defamatory," concluding that a wrong impression is equivalent to a falsehood.[49] Some courts have even gone so far as to rule that fiction which comes too close to reality could be a basis for a libel complaint.[50]

3. Opinion/Fair Comment An expression of opinion, as opposed to a statement of fact, is not a defamation.[51] For instance, one court ruled that "fraud" and "swindle" were colloquial words which could be used to describe a range of activities, and were therefore not false statements[52]. Another court ruled that "henchman" and "sleazy" were likewise opinion words.[53] Yet still another court ruled that use of the words "extortion" and "blackmail" was ambiguous and should be decided by a jury.[54] But editorial statements accusing a plaintiff of "amoral manipulation" and attempts to "shake down" elected officials have been ruled defamatory.[55] "Editorial hyperbole" was considered protected opinion by a court that also noted, "Some compression of facts relating to an item covered in a television broadcast is inevitable."[56]

Broadcasters and the print media may criticize all matters which are the subject of public controversy or are related to a matter of public interest. As long as there is no actual malice shown, defamatory comments by a broadcaster are protected under the "fair comment" privilege. It should be noted, however, that this protection extends only to matters of public concern. Thus, any intrusion into the activities of private persons, including the private life of a legitimate object of criticism, is not afforded the "fair comment" privilege. Opinions about public figures have been considered protected as forms of political debate.[57] However, opinion may sometimes be considered constitutionally protected only if the factual basis for the opinion is included so that others can draw their own conclusions.[58]

4. Public/Private Figures The principles which currently govern defamation law for the broadcast and print media have their roots in the 1964 New York Times decision.[59] There, the Supreme Court ruled that misstatements of fact, unjustified comments or opinions published by the media about the conduct of public officials were constitutionally privileged. Unless the false or unjustified material was published with "actual malice" (i.e. with actual knowledge of falsity or with reckless disregard of probable falsity), newspapers and broadcast stations could print or broadcast misstatements of fact about public officials without liability. Actual knowledge of falsity or reckless disregard of probable falsity must be proved by the injured party. This is an extremely difficult and sometimes impossible burden to meet.

This protection for the media against defamation liability was later expanded to include commentary on public figures,[60] and media coverage of all matters of public or general concern[61] -- even if the individual involved was a purely private person.

However, in 1974 this broad protection for the media was narrowed by the Supreme Court.[62] It ruled that the "actual malice" standard of the New York Times decision, while retaining its validity as to public officials and public figures, should not be forced on the states when a private individual is defamed, even when he is involved in an event of public interest. Rather than formulating a new rule itself, the Supreme Court allowed the 50 states to "define for themselves the appropriate standard of liability for a publisher or broadcaster of defamatory falsehoods injurious to a private individual."

Applying this Supreme Court direction, the various states have adopted differing standards of fault when a private individual or business entity is involved in a defamation action.[63] Therefore, careful scrutiny of local state law is suggested if a potential defamation occurs.

For example, a "simple negligence" standard has been applied in Arizona, California, District of Columbia, Florida, Hawaii, Illinois, Kansas, Kentucky, Maryland, Massachusetts, Ohio, Oklahoma, Pennsylvania,

Tennessee, Texas, Utah, Virginia and Washington.[64] New York has developed a "grossly irresponsible" test.[65] Alabama, Connecticut, Georgia, Iowa, Louisiana and Missouri have shown a tendency to adopt a standard requiring less than actual malice, but have not, as yet, specifically stated a rule.[66] Other states have retained the high standard of malice, but the definition of malice varies from state to state.

B. Defamation Based on Simple Negligence

A number of states now require a defamed person or business entity to prove only "simple negligence." However, the law in the state where the suit is brought must consider a corporate plaintiff to be a private and not a public entity.

In two 1979 opinions, the Supreme Court narrowed its definition of a public figure. In Wolston v. Reader's Digest Association,[67] the Court held that a limited-issue public figure must voluntarily enter a public controversy with the intent of affecting the outcome in order to be classified as a public figure. In Wolston, the Court ruled that an alleged spy who had been subpoenaed by a federal grand jury and failed to appear was not a public figure. His non-appearance was "in no way calculated to draw attention to himself in order to invite public comment or influence the public with respect to any issue."[68] In making its determination, the Court emphasized the need to examine the "nature and extent of an individual's participation in the particular controversy giving rise to the defamation."[69]

In Hutchinson v. Proxmire,[70] the Supreme Court held that a research scientist was not a public figure, regardless of the fact that he voluntarily applied for federal funding of his controversial research. The Court further noted that the plaintiff had no access to the media prior to the defamation and, therefore, could not be viewed as a public figure based on his access to the media after the defamation.

1. Corporate Plaintiffs Since 1979, the Supreme Court has denied review of several public figure cases,[71] and there is no clear pattern discernible at state trial court or appeals levels in the application of "private individual" status to business entities. One court concluded that a defense contractor was a "public figure" for the purposes of a libel suit.[72] The company claimed it had been libeled by a newspaper story about an alleged "stag party" held by corporate officials for Defense Department employees. The court stated that corporations were "...by definition, not private persons, and therefore do not require the...special protection afforded to individuals in protecting their private lives."

Another court ruled that corporations could be private entities entitled to the simple negligence standard in defamation actions, but declared one particular corporate plaintiff a public figure because it had been "drawn into a public controversy."[73] Here, the corporation claimed it had been libeled when the Associated Press printed incorrect reports that the Federal Trade Commission was about to charge the corporation with unfair and deceptive debt collecting practices. A similar analysis was followed when one court held that a corporate plaintiff, by reason of public financing activities, was a public figure for purposes of a libel suit.[74] Another court found a charitable corporation devoted to the humane treatment of animals to be a public figure.[75]

A U.S. Court of Appeals found a steak retailer to be a limited-purpose public figure because of its wide advertising campaign and its continuing access to channels of communication.[76] Similarly, in a Louisiana Court of Appeals, a carpet manufacturer and distributor was held to be a public figure. The court said that a business enterprise engaging in "extensive advertising...with the object of attracting prospective purchasers...and thereby increasing its sales and profit" is involved in matters of public concern.[77]

Other courts have taken contrary positions. In Arizona, for example, a court applied the "private individuals" approach and permitted an auto dealer to sue a newspaper for reporting that the dealer had the longest list of unresolved consumer complaints of any member of the local Better Business Bureau.[78] Similarly, a New York court ruled that a real estate corporation, erroneously identified as being involved in a land fraud inquiry, was to be treated as a private individual and could sue the Reader's Digest.[79] (However, the court ruled that the Reader's Digest's mistake stemmed from the plaintiff's similarity in name to the actual corporate wrongdoer, and the error was not gross negligence under New York law, or even simple negligence under Arizona law, because the magazine had no duty to investigate whether other companies existed with the same name.)

The view that corporations, as a class, are public figures is generally no longer followed.[80] In an action involving a corporation engaged in the production of commercial fishing boats, the court held that the corporation was not a public figure even though it publicly advertised its products, and even though defects in boats manufactured by the plaintiff were the subject of a public controversy.[81] In that case, the First Circuit applied a two-step analysis which has since been adopted by other courts.[82] The court initially attempted to determine whether a controversy existed and if it preceded the alleged defamation. Finding that a controversy did not precede publication, the court then attempted to determine to what extent the plaintiff had voluntarily participated in the controversy giving rise to the defamation.

Other courts have suggested that in determining whether a plaintiff is a public figure, the court should evaluate two additional factors. First, did the plaintiff voluntarily assume the increased risk of defamation that accompanies fame? And secondly, did the plaintiff have a greater access to the media than a private individual would possess?[83] An affirmative response to either of these questions could warrant a public figure classification.[84]

In some decisions, the courts have mentioned the size of the corporate plaintiffs when ruling on whether the corporation is a private or public entity. In deeming Martin Marietta and Reliance Insurance Company public entities, for example, the courts specifically mentioned the size of those corporations, whereas, in holding that Trans World Accounts, Inc. was a private entity, the court noted that it was "not large enough to automatically be considered a public figure."[85]

Several plaintiffs have been treated as public figures by trial courts, but have been awarded private figure status on appeal. An archaeological consulting firm retained by a local government agency was ruled by a U.S. Court of Appeals to be neither a public figure (since it did not press itself into a public controversy), nor a public official (since it had no control over government).[86] One retail firm conducted a widely publicized close-out sale in the controversial closing of a prominent department store. The firm was held on appeal to be a private figure because it was merely doing business with the real parties to the public controversy.[87] A well-known luxury resort and its owners both were declared private figures on appeal because neither had voluntarily thrown themselves into public controversy.[88]

In sum, in those states where an action for defamation can be based on simple negligence, a corporation could have a significantly easier standard of proof in cases involving the broadcast media. The standard of simple negligence could be met by establishing that the broadcaster did not use reasonable care in attempting to broadcast an accurate and fair comment. However, this easier standard only applies if the corporation is held to be a private figure, and the court's ruling on public/private status may be difficult to predict.

C. Defamation Based on Malice

If a business entity is deemed a public figure, then actual malice must be established. Actual malice is defined to be the publication of material "with knowledge that it was false or with reckless disregard of whether it was false or not."[89] Application of this definition has varied.

The Supreme Court has held that actual malice could only be found in the following types of situations:

(i) Where the false statements are made with a "high degree of awareness of their probable falsity" (emphasis added);[90]

(ii) Where there is "highly unreasonable conduct constituting an extreme departure from the standards of investigation and reporting ordinarily adhered to by responsible publishers" (emphasis added);[91] and

(iii) Where there is "sufficient evidence to permit the conclusion that the defendant in fact entertained serious doubts as to the truth of his publication."[92]

It should be noted that the term "actual malice" is a term of art and does not have the traditional meaning of the word "malice". Therefore, ill will, spite, hatred, hostility, a deliberate intention to harm or some sinister or corrupt motive are constitutionally insufficent to establish "actual malice."[93] Rather, actual knowledge of falsity or a reckless disregard of whether the statements were false must be shown. Because of the extreme difficulty of meeting this standard of proof, the vast majority of defamation cases against the media are dismissed on motions for summary judgment, and never get to trial.

1. Recent Trends However, several cases have demonstrated a softening of this hard line. Certain conduct of investigative reporters may be so unreasonable as to indicate the presence of "actual malice."

For example, one decision involved published statements that a plaintiff was covertly financed and supported by government agencies, including the Pentagon and Central Intelligence Agency. In light of the fact that the defamatory matter was published after strong denials by CIA officials, the court stated:

> But while it is well established that a failure to investigate, without more, is insufficient to give rise to liability, once one has undertaken to conduct an investigation he should not be permitted to ignore with impunity the fruits of that investigation. (emphasis added)94

Thus, the court held that actual malice could be established if the media report was in conflict with facts obtained during its investigation.

In another case, the former mayor of San Francisco brought a libel action seeking damages for an expose of his alleged relationship with organized crime. The broadcaster knew of sources to verify the information, but did not contact those sources. In applying the actual malice standard, the court stated:

> While New York Times imposes no liability for failure to verify the accuracy of reports, the failure to pursue what appears to have been the most obvious available source of possible corroboration must, under all of the circumstances of this case, be regarded as clear and convincing evidence of reckless disregard for the truth.[95]

Thus, actual malice can be established if the broadcaster ignores "the most obvious available source."

Another case involved a libel action against a television station and a reporter for their 5:30 and 11:00 p.m. news reports that "reliable sources" had implicated the mayor in an extortion and embezzlement scheme.[96] In overturning the lower court's directed verdict for the broadcasters, the court noted that the "reliable sources" were completely anonymous to the reporter. That fact, coupled with the reporter's failure to acknowledge the mayor's denial and assertion of the story's falsity in the 11:00 p.m. broadcast, could have supported a jury finding of actual malice. The court stated that "anonymous sources or otherwise suspect sources should be verified."

A third decision representative of this trend held a newspaper and its employees guilty of reckless disregard of whether charges against a building official were true or false. They published the articles with a high degree of awareness of the probable falsity of the statements involved.[97] The court stated that despite awareness of a number of facts which strongly suggested the plaintiff's innocence, the articles were nonetheless written "in the face of all those red flags flying." In this case, the jury ultimately awarded damages in the amount of $114,000 (compensatory) and $1,000,000 (punitive).

Other media actions found to constitute malice include failing to corroborate facts overheard from one side of a telephone conversation,[98] neglecting to independently check the accuracy of a statement made by a state official in a press conference,[99] and relying solely on the statements of an informant when there were "obvious reasons" to doubt his veracity.[100] In a libel suit against a newspaper, one state supreme court ruled that previously published erroneous articles having no relationship to the case at hand are evidence of malice.[101] Prompt retraction of an allegedly libelous statement does not indicate a lack of malice.[102]

2. Proving Actual Malice A 1979 Supreme Court decision in the defamation law area could have a significant impact on the ability of a plaintiff to prove actual malice in a libel suit against the media. In Herbert v. Lando,[103] the Court ruled on the question of whether, and to what extent, the plaintiff could question a television producer about how an allegedly defamatory "60 Minutes" segment was put together. The producer claimed that his conclusions concerning the credibility of sources he had interviewed; decisions he had made in pursuing leads or not investigating certain matters; reasons for those conclusions; and discussions on what would be excluded from or included in the final program were all protected from disclosure on First Amendment grounds because they were part of the "editorial process." The plaintiff argued that this information was critical to showing a newsman's state

of mind and was the essence of proving actual malice. The Court agreed with the plaintiff and held as follows:

> When a member of the press is alleged to have circulated damaging falsehoods and is sued for injury to the plaintiff's reputation, there is no privilege under the First Amendment's guarantee of freedom of speech and freedom of press barring the plaintiff from inquiring into the editorial process of those responsible for the publication where the inquiry will produce evidence material to the proof of a critical element of the plaintiff's cause of action.

As a result of this ruling, evidence of actual malice in suits against the media may be less difficult to obtain.

3. Corporations May Be Sued The development of the law in this respect has not been restricted to suits against the media. In a 1977 California decision, the situation was reversed. A representative of television station KNBC sued Pacific Gas & Electric Company for defamation.[104]

KNBC had produced and broadcast a documentary on nuclear power which included interviews with employees of the utility company. The company denounced the documentary in a document which was sent to a number of people, including government officials. (Thus, there was publication by the company to the same legal extent as a statement broadcast over a station or appearing in a newspaper.) KNBC asserted that a number of charges in the document were false and that the company acted with a reckless disregard for the truth.

The court ruled that the company could be held liable for defamation. Actual malice could be shown because the company was aware of the seriousness of the charges, made little or no investigation of their veracity, and had attempted to suppress the broadcast of the documentary. This case also illustrates that a corporation must be extremely careful in the actions it takes in reaction to an allegedly defamatory broadcast, or the company itself may become liable for defamation.[105]

4. Neutral Reporting As a Media Defense The media can sometimes avoid liability for publishing or broadcasting defamatory comments, even though actual malice might be attributable to the source of the comment. This is the principle of "neutral reportage" developed in a recent case by the Second Circuit Court of Appeals.[106]

In that case, the Audubon Society attacked the integrity of distinguished scientists who had taken a position on the effect of DDT on the environment. A New York Times article reported that an Audubon official said the scientists were "lying" and were "paid to lie." The Times reporter admitted that he had "serious doubts about the truth" of those charges.

The court held that the New York Times could not be held liable for these apparently defamatory statements because the court did "...not believe that the press may be required under the First Amendment to suppress newsworthy statements merely because it has serious doubts regarding their truth."[107] The court held that the statement was "newsworthy" because a "responsible, prominent organization like the National Audubon Society" made serious charges against public officials. The court cautioned, however, that the media must be neutral in their reporting and could be held liable if they espouse the charges, deliberately distort the statements, or undertake a personal attack of their own.

Thus, neutral reportage of defamatory but newsworthy charges involving public figures, generated by a responsible source, may exempt the media from liability for libel, even though the media have "serious doubts regarding their truth." Of course, the person or entity originally making the charges would be subject to liability for defamation.

D. Corporate Officers, Corporate Management and Corporate Products and Services

1. Status of Corporate Officers Courts have been inconsistent in deciding the status of corporate officers

who sue for defamation. Some courts have held that a corporate officer will have the same status as his corporate employer if there is a connection between the subject matter of the misstatement and his corporate responsibilities.[108] Other courts have not tied the status of corporate officers to that of their corporations.[109]

It is clear, however, that in most states a corporate official will be considered a private individual for defamation purposes and held to a simple negligence standard of proof, providing the misstatement does not relate to his official corporate conduct. For example, a former airline vice president was held to be a private individual when referred to in a magazine article one and one-half years after he was fired.[110] In another decision, a high executive in a "Top 100" corporation was not considered a public figure when a defamatory article concerning him was published in a business news publication.[111] In ruling that he was a private individual for purposes of the defamation suit, the court made the following significant observations:

(i) He held no public office;

(ii) He did not have general fame or notoriety in the community;

(iii) He had no pervasive involvement in public affairs; and

(iv) He had not injected himself into a public controversy.

However, if the libel does relate to the official's corporate position, he may be required to show malice. The former president of a large consumer cooperative was held to be a public figure for the limited purpose of comment about the financial status of the business.[112] A nursing home owner was ruled neither a public official nor a public figure, but was still required to prove malice in reports about the nursing home because he was engaged in a "public interest" business.[113]

2. Product Disparagement If the defamation does not involve the corporation itself or the corporate officers, but rather a product of the corporation, it may be possible to bring a product disparagement action. Disparagement of products or disparagement of title has been defined as an untrue publication, made without privilege or justification, which disparages another's product or service under circumstances that would lead a reasonably prudent potential purchaser to refuse to purchase the product or service.[114]

Generally, although the terminology differs from state to state, the necessary elements of a product disparagement claim are: (1) publication; (2) falsity (must be an actual misstatement of fact, as opposed to opinion); (3) disparaging; (4) forseeable injury; (5) pecuniary loss from impaired sales (there must be a showing of actual damages); and (6) lack of privilege.

Those states applying the "simple negligence" standard in defamation cases will utilize a similar rule in product disparagement. Therefore, no actual malice need be shown. States adhering to the New York Times standard require actual malice.

Usually, actual damages is the most difficult element to prove in a product disparagement action, and cases often fail for this reason. This has occurred where the management of a taxi fleet was accused of permitting its drivers to cheat out-of-town customers,[115] where a television station incorrectly reported that key personnel of a restaurant had departed,[116] and where a radio station disparaged a company by stating that its competition was the only company of its kind.[117]

E. Retraction Statutes

A number of states have retraction statutes which generally allow a broadcaster to escape some of the liability for a defamatory broadcast if he airs a timely retraction. Often these statutes will preclude awarding general or punitive damages in a libel suit if the retraction is broadcast, allowing instead only special damages (proof of actual economic loss).

California, for example, limits recovery to special damages unless (within 20 days after knowledge of the broadcast) the complainant serves the station with a written document specifying the statements claimed to be libelous and demanding that those statements be corrected.[118] Other state statutes do not directly limit damages. Some merely provide that a retraction may be considered mitigating,[119] or may tend to negate the inference of malice.[120] Of extreme importance are those state statutes that make a demand for retraction a condition precedent to the bringing of a suit.[121] In other words, failure to demand the retraction would bar a plaintiff from suing for defamation in those states.

Another distinguishing factor in these statutes is the extent to which they protect specific persons or media. For instance, some retraction statutes apply to publication in newspapers or magazines, to radio and television broadcasts, or any combination thereof.[122] Others deal with the protection of specific classes of individuals involved with the media, such as licensees, reporters and writers.[123]

It must be remembered that federal courts apply state law in libel actions. Therefore, it is imperative that the applicable state statutes be checked in a timely manner if a potential defamation occurs.

F. Conclusion

The present state of the law of defamation may be summarized as follows:

(i) There is immunity from liability for defamation based upon pure comment or opinion;

(ii) Actual knowledge of falsity, or reckless disregard of probable falsity, will subject the media to liability for libel of public officials and public figures, including individuals who voluntarily thrust themselves into the vortex of a public issue;

(iii) The media may be held liable for libel of private individuals if, with fault, the publication (broadcast) contains a false statement of fact which poses a substantial danger to reputation, on its face;

(iv) Each state may determine the appropriate fault standard of liability for defamatory falsehood injurious to a private individual, but the states may not impose liability without fault;

(v) Neutral reportage of newsworthy charges involving public figures, made by a responsible source, may be immune from liability even if the reporter has personal doubts as to their truth; and

(vi) Retraction statutes may reduce the liability of the broadcaster.

II. Right of Privacy

Corporate officers may be able to challenge the broadcast of facts about their private lives as an invasion of privacy. The applicability of a right of privacy action is limited, however, and often depends on the present newsworthiness of the information disclosed.

There are traditionally four categories of invasion of privacy:

(i) Placing a person in a false light;

(ii) Publication of embarrassing private facts about a person;

(iii) Intrusion upon a person's seclusion or solitude; and

(iv) Misappropriation of a person's personality for commercial benefit.

Although privacy actions are generally unavailable for corporations, corporate officers may be able to successfully challenge the broadcast of certain facts about themselves. The elements of a privacy action will be briefly set out, and then the limitations on this action for corporations and corporate officers will be explored.

A. Placing a Person in a False Light

This usually results from a report's fictionalization, expansion or embellishment of the truth. The underlying facts may be basically sound, but the embellishment gives a false impression as to the person's character or the subject matter of the report. This could also occur where the omission of facts changes the general import of the report.

B. Publication of Embarrassing Private Facts

An invasion of privacy exists where the extent of the intimate details reported does not further the newsworthiness of the event with which the private facts are associated. This is often the case where, in reporting on a recent newsworthy development in the life of a public figure, the reporter digs up intimate details of the person's past life unrelated to the present event.

C. Intrusion

Intrusion means either actual physical intrusion into the individual's home or the use of mechanical devices, binoculars or tapes, to oversee or overhear the individual's private affairs. Surreptitious photographing and recording in the course of news gathering may give rise to a privacy action based on intrusion.

D. Misappropriation of Personality

This generally refers to the use of a person's name, portrait or picture for advertising purposes, or for the purposes of trade, without consent of the individual. This type of invasion of privacy can often be unintentional. For example, a picture of a tombstone, with the name of the deceased clearly readable, was used in a television advertisement for a tombstone manufacturer.

E. Corporate Privacy

Private matters of a business nature are not protected by the right of privacy as developed by U.S. courts. The right of privacy is designed to protect personal feelings and sensibilities rather than business or pecuniary interests, and accordingly, such protection has been denied when asserted by corporations.[124] For example, in an action challenging the power of the Federal Trade Commission to require a corporation to file certain compliance reports, the Supreme Court stated that corporations could claim no equality with individuals in the enjoyment of the right of privacy.[125]

Although a corporate officer is entitled to a right of privacy, the availability of a right of privacy action is limited. This limitation is similar to that imposed in the area of defamation. If an individual is a public figure, or is involved in a newsworthy occurrence, then he implicitly waives his right to privacy. Therefore, publication of private facts relating to a person's capacity as a corporate officer would probably not be grounds for a successful right of privacy action. On the other hand, publication of private facts unrelated to a person's corporate office might be successfully challenged on privacy grounds.

III. The Right to Gather News as it Affects Corporations

The First Amendment does not immunize a newsman from tortious conduct, such as trespass, while gathering news. The First Amendment does, however, in some cases allow newsmen to protect confidential sources when subpoenaed in civil and criminal cases. Assertion of this privilege by a newsman may prevent a party from obtaining valuable information.

A. Introduction

There is no legally recognized "right" of the media to gather news, but the concept of a right to gather news is relevant to corporations in several respects. One question raised is the extent to which the First Amendment immunizes newsmen from tortious conduct while gathering news. (It doesn't.) Another area of concern derives from the fact that the ability to gather news is the foundation on which journalists, including broadcasters, assert a privilege to refuse to disclose confidential information when subpoenaed in civil and criminal proceedings.

For the corporation, a claim of newsman's privilege could arise in a criminal proceeding brought against it. Often prosecutions result from news articles on a corporation's activities. If the corporation seeks information from the reporter (i.e. notes, sources and the like), it might be faced with a claim of privilege.

Claims of confidentiality of sources or background material might also be raised to frustrate a corporation's attempt to obtain information in a defamation suit against a newspaper or broadcaster. The privilege may also arise in a civil lawsuit to which a corporation is a party and the media, while not parties, have information relevant to a claim or defense.

These two elements of newsgathering -- the newsman's privilege against disclosure and the claim of First Amendment immunization against liability for tortious conduct -- are analyzed in the following section of this report.

B. Newsman's Privilege

1. Common Law Background At common law, there was no recognition of a privilege against source disclosure.[126] A journalist could be compelled to reveal his sources when subpoenaed to testify before a grand jury, court or legislature.[127] The theory was that every man owed his testimony when called to give evidence.[128] While non-disclosure privileges existed as exceptions to this general rule (e.g. attorney-client), the tendency was to restrict such privileges.[129]

Generally, courts held that a reporter could not invoke a privilege to refuse to answer pertinent questions relating to communications made to him as a reporter.

2. Constitutional Dimensions The common law has been substantially modified by court decisions construing the First Amendment. In analyzing these decisions, it is necessary to keep in mind that distinctions are made between the criminal and civil context. In light of the varying interests at stake, courts are less likely to uphold claims of privilege in criminal proceedings than in civil cases.[130]

First Amendment protection for confidential sources was first sought in a defamation suit. The court held that a columnist had no First Amendment right to refuse to answer relevant questions concerning his sources because the information sought went to the very heart of the plaintiff's claim.[131]

The constitutional aspects of the newsman's privilege subsequently arose in a criminal prosecution involving three cases where reporters refused to testify at grand jury proceedings, claiming that the confidentiality of their sources was protected by the First Amendment.[132] The Supreme Court held that the First Amendment freedom of the press did not guarantee a reporter the right to keep the identity of a confidential source from a grand jury. But the Court did not flatly deny the possibility of such a privilege either.

Thereafter, many criminal cases involved situations where a defendant sought confidential sources or background information from journalists. Here, the reporter's privilege clashed with the defendant's right to a fair trial. The judicial trend which developed was to balance the defendant's need for the information against the newsman's need for confidentiality.[133] Thus, the party seeking disclosure in criminal proceedings was required to establish (1) that the information was not available from another source, (2) that it was of unquestioned materiality and relevance, and (3) that the defendant's need outweighed the privilege.

In the civil context, most courts required that the party seeking disclosure demonstrate (1) that the information went to the heart of the claim, (2) that it could not be obtained through alternative means, and (3) that the need for the information was sufficiently compelling to overcome First Amendment protections.[134]

The trend toward a qualified privilege in both civil and criminal proceedings was interrupted in 1978 by a highly publicized decision which concerned Myron Farber, a reporter for the New York Times. Farber wrote several stories that led to the murder indictment and prosecution of Dr. Mario Jascalevich.[135]

During the trial, Farber refused to comply with a subpoena by the defense for his notes. He then refused to obey an order for a private inspection of his notes by the trial judge. Farber was found guilty of contempt of court. He sought a stay of his sentence from Justices White and Marshall of the Supreme Court. Justice White denied the stay, stating:

> There is no present authority in this court either that newsmen are constitutionally privileged to withhold duly subpoenaed documents material to the prosecution or defense of a criminal case or that a defendant seeking the subpoena must show extraordinary circumstances before enforcement against newsmen will be had.[136]

The case was returned to the New Jersey Supreme Court. It rejected Farber's claim that the First Amendment required a balancing of the defendant's need for the information against the reporter's need for confidentiality. Farber was precluded from asserting the newsman's privilege of confidentiality.

Since the Farber decision, courts have been sharply divided over whether to adopt the concept of a qualified newsman's privilege or to totally eliminate the privilege in criminal cases. Some lower courts have held that reporters lack any privilege under the First Amendment.[137] Others, however, continue to rule that a qualified privilege exists.[138] The law in criminal cases can only be resolved in the Supreme Court, and the Supreme Court has not yet acted.[139]

The Farber case has not had the same divisive impact in the civil context that has been found in criminal proceedings. Cases since Farber continue to recognize a qualified newsman's privilege in civil proceedings.[140] All circuit courts that have considered the question have ruled that a qualified privilege should be readily available in civil actions.[141]

Of course, even if a qualified privilege is recognized, the facts of a given case may require that the privilege yield. For example, when a public figure brings an action for defamation, he must prove actual malice on the part of the broadcaster, and the plaintiff may need background material or the identity of a source to do so. The Supreme Court decision in Herbert v. Lando is instructive on this point. The Court held that the First Amendment did not bar a public figure from probing the editorial process of a broadcaster in order to prove actual malice.[142]

Some state courts have demanded even more. A Hawaii state court ordered a reporter to reveal the identity of sources which were central to a libel suit brought by a businessman against a local television station.[143] A New Mexico state court ordered a similar disclosure of sources in a libel action, as well as all notes and documents relating to the plaintiff, including information which was not used as the basis for any of the articles in question.[144] The Massachusetts Supreme Court ruled that reporters have no qualified privilege, even if the information desired is irrelevant or available from other sources.[145]

Thus, in a defamation proceeding, there is some chance that a newsman or reporter may not be permitted to retain confidentiality of his notes and sources, if the disclosure of this information will assist the individual or corporate plaintiff in establishing malice.

Other courts have ruled that the refusal to disclose a source will be presumed to mean that there was no source. The assumption would severely hamper a defense against the charge of malice.[146]

3. Shield Laws The inadequacies of judicial protection at common law led many states to enact shield laws which allow journalists to refuse disclosure of their sources under certain circumstances. Prior to 1972, shield laws had been enacted in 17 states.[147] By 1979, at least 26 states had enacted some form of privilege.[148] In 1980, California became the first state to incorporate a shield law into its state constitution, in a proposition which the state's voters approved by a 3-1 margin.[149] This new, stronger law has been upheld by both a state court and a federal district court.[150] The effect of shield laws is by no means certain. Courts have given widely divergent constructions to such laws. In some cases, shield laws have been severely narrowed in their scope on constitutional grounds, such as the right to a fair trial.[151] In other cases, the laws have been used successfully by the media. In an elections dispute, one state court applied the state's shield law by ordering a reporter to produce some of his notes while also giving him discretion to withhold whatever information he considered confidential.[152] In Pennsylvania, a federal appeals court applied the state shield law to prevent a meat retailer from obtaining a television station's outtakes in a federal libel case.[153] Similarly, a federal court in New York invoked an out-of-state shield law to protect a newspaper's sources in a libel suit involving an insurance company.[154]

A corporation faced with a journalist's assertion of privilege must look to the law of relevant jurisdiction. The success of a corporation's attempt to obtain sources and background material will depend on the specific law where the proceeding is brought, and the court's application of that law.

C. Newsgathering and Tortious Conduct

Another serious issue affecting corporations is the extent to which the First Amendment immunizes the media from liability for wrongs committed during newsgathering. Such tortious conduct might consist of harassment, trespassing, wiretapping, assault or battery. Only a few decisions have dealt specifically with this issue. These cases have uniformly rejected the contention that the First Amendment serves to immunize a newsman from liability for such conduct.

For example, one court found against a photographer whose constant surveillance, and obtrusive and intruding presence went beyond the bounds of reasonable newsgathering.[155] The court, therefore, granted an injunction. However, it distinguished that photographer's excessive behavior from other photographers' reasonable efforts to report on the plaintiff.

In a California case, two reporters, acting in concert with the police, posed as prospective patients and gained entrance to the plaintiff's home. The court ruled that the reporters' photography and recording of the plaintiff, without his consent, resulted in emotional distress. The plaintiff won his suit for invasion of privacy.[156] The court stated that the First Amendment is not a license to trespass, steal or intrude by electronic means into another's home or office.

A Florida decision held that a reporter's entry into a burned-out private home, at the invitation of police and fire officials, and in accordance with accepted custom, did not constitute an unlawful trespass. The case was based on an implied consent theory.[157] In addition, the stories and photographs, which were not false or inaccurate, were held not to constitute an invasion of privacy.

Of potentially great significance to a corporation is a 1978 New York case holding that the First Amendment has <u>never</u> been construed to provide newsmen with immunity for torts or crimes committed during newsgathering. In that case, a restaurant sued successfully for a trespass by a television crew that, after the restaurant was cited for health code violations, entered the restaurant "with cameras rolling" to do a story.[158]

These opinions may signify the development of a trend that will afford a corporation protection from unwarranted intrusion by the news media.

IV. Damages

Money damages are the prime remedy awarded by the courts when a defamation, privacy violation or trespass is proven. Therefore, a brief discussion of the kinds of damages which may be available to an individual or corporate plaintiff follows. These damages include general damages, actual or special damages, and punitive damages.

A. General Damages

General damages may be awarded for harm presumed to have occurred as a result of the libel. Juries traditionally have been allowed to award substantial sums as compensation for supposed injury to reputation, without any proof that such harm actually occurred. But in libel actions involving the media, the Supreme Court has severely limited general damages for two reasons: (1) the largely uncontrolled discretion of juries to award damages where there was no loss inhibited the vigorous exercise of First Amendment freedoms by the media, and (2) the doctrine of presumed damages invited juries to punish unpopular opinion rather than to compensate individuals for injuries sustained by the publication of a false fact. The Court held that unless actual malice on the part of the media could be shown, damages must be limited to compensation for actual injury.[159]

B. Actual Damages

Under present law, some real injury or loss must be shown in most cases before a plaintiff can collect money damages in a defamation suit against the media. Usually, this would mean a showing of pecuniary loss by the plaintiff. However, awards of special or actual damages are not always limited to out-of-pocket loss. Impairment of reputation and standing in the community, personal humiliation, and mental anguish or suffering may also be the basis for actual damages. Still, the injury must be proven and may not be presumed.[160]

C. Punitive Damages

Punitive damages are awarded to punish the defendant for his wrongful act in defaming the plaintiff, and to deter others, as well as the defendant, from similar conduct in the future. Fear of huge jury awards unnecessarily inhibits the media in exercising their First Amendment freedoms. Therefore, the Supreme Court has restricted punitive damages awards to cases in which a plaintiff proves actual malice, i.e., that the media had knowledge of the falsity of their statements, or acted in reckless disregard as to their falsity.[161] One court held that a state statute authorizing punitive damages did not conflict with the First Amendment. In that case, a libel action was brought by a public figure and actual malice was established. The court found the state had a compelling interest in deterring malicious defamation and that, therefore, punitive damages were warranted.[162]

Recent examples of damages awards include a case in which an insurance company lost its entire agency force because of a defamation and was required to hire and train additional agents. In this case, a court held that a $1.9-million award was not excessive.[163]

The potential for sizable awards encourages plaintiffs to seek punitive damages in addition to actual damages. A former beauty contest winner was recently awarded a total of $26.5 million for a libelous article appearing in a national magazine.[164] One popular entertainer was awarded $1.6 million for comments made in a gossip column.[165]

While punitive damages may sometimes be available, in most cases it is necessary for the plaintiff to prove actual pecuniary loss. In the business context, such losses might include lost sales directly tied to the defamatory broadcast, or advertising costs of overcoming the false impression of the broadcast. If a potential defamation of an individual, business entity or product occurs, it is important that the person or business immediately begin to carefully document any losses or expenses which are incurred as a result of the alleged defamation.

CONCLUSION

This report has given an overview of the remedies available to private citizens and commercial entities when a radio or television station broadcasts information which is biased, distorted, or untrue.

Administrative remedies before the Federal Communications Commission -- including Fairness Doctrine, personal attack, political broadcasting, and news distortion — have the benefits of being relatively inexpensive and simple to pursue. Because radio and television stations must constantly be aware of protecting their licenses granted by the Commission, broadcasters are particularly sensitive to complaints addressed to the Commission. Therefore a station may choose to resolve a complaint amicably and quickly to avoid protracted Commission proceedings that may affect its license. However, should the station choose to resist the complaint, there are substantial detriments to proceedings before the Commission. There is no right to discovery; the burden of proof is almost exclusively on the complainant; substantial time elapses before a decision is rendered; and, for the most part, the remedies are inadequate. Unless a flagrant abuse of the rules is shown, the Commission will usually defer to the broadcaster's judgment in meeting the obligations discussed above. Even if the Commission does act to censure the licensee, the station still has wide discretion as to how it will respond in its on-the-air programming.

Judicial relief is generally found in the law of defamation, although some right-of-privacy actions may also be helpful. The media generally enjoy a high degree of protection against liability for broadcasting untrue comments. A broadcaster may not be held liable for untrue statements about a public official or a public figure unless the broadcast is made with actual malice (*i.e.* with knowledge that the statement was false, or made with reckless disregard of whether it was false or not). Proving actual malice is very difficult for a plaintiff, and the vast majority of defamation cases against the media are thrown out without ever going to trial, because actual malice cannot be proved. However, several recent cases demonstrate a softening of this hard line. These cases indicate that some conduct of investigative reporters is so unreasonable that it cannot be given the broad protection previously extended. Such unreasonable activities include ignoring the fruits of an investigation, and the failure to pursue obvious sources of corroboration.

When the plaintiff is a private individual (not a public figure) many states allow recovery from the media if it can be shown that the broadcaster was merely negligent in broadcasting the untrue statement. This is significantly easier for a plaintiff to prove than the actual malice required of public figure plaintiffs. In most cases, however, large corporate plaintiffs would probably be held to be public figures and face the higher standard of proof. Most states also have retraction statutes that significantly influence the damages which a libel plaintiff may obtain. Since each state has different laws in the defamation area, it is extremely important to consider carefully the laws of the particular state where the defamation suit is to be brought.

Closely related to defamation suits are right-of-privacy actions. This right of action is generally available to individuals, including corporate officers. However, it is not available to a corporation itself.

The law concerning the privileges and restrictions of newsmen is rapidly changing. At present it can be said that the First Amendment does not protect newsmen from lawsuits over wrongs committed when gathering news. But it does allow newsmen some degree of protection of their confidential sources when subpoenaed in civil and criminal cases.

The remedy for defamation, invasion of privacy, or tortious conduct by the media is damages. In most media cases, the plaintiff will be required to prove actual loss or injury in order to prevail. However, if it can be shown that the media acted with actual malice, a court could also award general damages (damages which are presumed without proof) or punitive damages, to punish the defendant and deter similar conduct in the future.

In choosing between administrative and judicial remedies, the individual or the corporation should consider what type of redress is desired. A complaint to the Federal Communications Commission could result in the airing of other viewpoints on a controversial issue (under the Fairness Doctrine) or the opportunity for a personal response (under the personal attack and political broadcasting rules). The Commission can neither award monetary compensation for injury, nor can it order reimbursement of attorney's fees. A civil court suit may result in a monetary award for damages, but will not affect the public's awareness of differing views on an issue. The situations eligible for redress in each case are restricted. For example, the Fairness Doctrine and the personal attack rules are applicable only to issues of public controversy, and news broadcasts are exempt from the personal attack rules. On the other hand, a libel suit is applicable only to false statements of fact, not unfavorable expressions of opinion. Therefore, the circumstances of the offending broadcast and the type of relief sought will determine the route chosen. Of course, administrative and judicial remedies can be pursued simultaneously.

The chances for success before the Commission or the courts are not good. The Federal Communications Commission reports receiving 4,490 Fairness Doctrine complaints in fiscal 1979; 9,897 in 1980; and 5,932 in 1981. Only about 30 complaints a year led to station inquiries, and violations of the Fairness Doctrine were found in only five cases in 1979, four in 1980, and one in 1981.[166] Even when a violation is found, a television station generally has much leeway in correcting it. Commission action usually takes the form of a warning to the station, "not to let it happen again," or an order for the station to advise the Commission within 20 days on how it plans to change its policy to correct the situation. However, a corporation's notification to a television station that it plans to file a complaint with the Commission may act as a spur to negotiations so that an agreement can be reached without formal action.

The success rate for judicial remedies is equally discouraging. A Stanford law professor has compiled a study analyzing all reported libel cases involving the media (print and broadcast) in both state and federal courts between January 1977 and September 1980, a total of 291 cases.[167] The study shows that the media defendants won 66 percent of all cases, while the plaintiffs prevailed in only 5 percent. (The remainder produced indeterminate results). Of the 190 cases that went to the appellate level, business corporations were involved in 10 percent, and business owners or managers in 17 percent. Only one of the corporations and only two of the business owners or managers prevailed. Television stations and networks did not lose a single case at either the trial or appellate level.

This study provided other informative statistics. Juries were much more likely than judges to find for the plaintiff. State and federal defenses played an approximately equal role in the media defendants' successes overall, but state defenses were used more often to defeat corporations and managers. The media are least successful in the states known as the "group of nine" (Alabama, Alaska, California, Florida, Hawaii, New Hampshire, Oklahoma, South Carolina and Vermont).[168] Media defendants are most successful (93 percent of the time) in Illinois because of that state's unique "innocent construction rule."[169]

Of course, plaintiffs in libel cases may be somewhat more successful than the study indicates, because out-of-court settlements do not show up among reported cases. For example, data from one libel insurer indicates that of 110 cases closed in 1979, 25 were dropped by the plaintiff, 30 were settled for payments ranging from $300 to $50,000, and 55 were litigated.[170] However, the study concludes that "even if unreported settlements play as great a role as some preliminary data suggest, suits against media defendants are not likely to be rewarding."[171]

In the future, judicial remedies may offer more hope for the plaintiff. Results of a survey of 86 libel lawyers in 24 states indicate that most believe the constitutional protections enjoyed by the media against libel suits will diminish during this decade.[172]

Administrative remedies, on the other hand, may cease to be available at all. In the current de-regulatory climate, both government and private sector forces are pressing Congress to repeal the Fairness Doctrine, personal attack and political broadcasting rules.

TABLE OF CITATIONS

1. Broadcasters have a statutory obligation under the Communications Act to comply with the Fairness Doctrine. Both radio and TV broadcasters are affected, despite the recent substantial "deregulation" of radio.

2. Compare Red Lion Broadcasting Co. v. FCC, 381 F.2d 908 (D.C. Cir. 1967) and Tornillo v. Miami Herald, 287 So.2d 78 (Fla. Sup. Ct. 1973).

3. 59 FCC 2d 987 (1976).

4. Broadcast Procedure Manual, 49 FCC 2d 1 (1974) at 5.

5. National Citizens Committee for Broadcasting v. FCC, 567 F.2d 1095, at 1111 (D.C. Cir. 1977), cert. denied, 436 U.S. 926 (1978); Democractic National Committee v. FCC, 460 F.2d 891, (D.C. Cir. 1972) at 911, cert. denied, 409 U.S. 843 (1972).

6. Broadcast Procedure Manual, 49 FCC 2d 1 (1974) at 5.

7. See also, Allen C. Phelps, 21 FCC 2d 12 (1960); Reconsideration of Fairness Report, 58 FCC 2d 691 (1976) at 696, quoting Fairness Doctrine Primer, 40 FCC 2d 582 (1973) at 600.

8. Peter C. Herbst, 48 FCC 2d 614 (1974) at 615, aff'd., sub nom., Public Interest Research Group v. FCC, 522 F.2d 1060 (1975), cert. denied, 424 U.S. 965 (1976).

9. A corporation might seek relief through the Federal Trade Commission if it feels it has been maligned by a false or deceptive advertisement. However, in 1980 Congress ruled that Federal Trade Commission inquiries should not extend to "unfair" advertisements.

10. Public Media Center, 59 FCC 2d 494 (1976), reconsid. denied, 64 FCC 2d 615 (1977), remanded on other grounds, 587 F.2d 1322 (D.C. Cir. 1978); on remand, 72 FCC 2d 776 (1979).

11. Energy Action Committee, 64 FCC 2d 787 (1977).

12. Public Media Center, supra., fn. 10.

13. Environmental Defense Fund et al. v. KERO-TV et al., 90 FCC 2d 648 (1982).

14. Cf. FCC treatment of corporate "issue ads" discussed infra.

15. Columbia Broadcasting System, Inc. v. Democratic National Committee, 412 U.S. 94 (1973).

16. Accuracy in Media, Inc., 40 FCC 2d 958 (1973), applic. for review denied, 44 FCC 2d 1027 (1973), rev'd. sub nom.; National Broadcasting Co. v. FCC, 516 F.2d 1101 (D.C. Cir. 1974), reversal vacated and rehearing granted at 1155; rehearing en banc vacated at 1156; second reversal vacated as moot and remanded with direction to vacate initial order and dismiss complaint at 1180.

17. Public Media Center, supra., fn. 10.

18. In re Wilderness Society, 31 FCC 2d 729 (1971), reconsid. denied, 32 FCC 2d 714 (1971).

19. American Security Council Educational Foundation v. FCC, 607 F.2d 438 (D.C. Cir. 1979), cert. denied, 444 U.S. 1013 (1980).

20. American Security Council Educational Foundation v. FCC, 63 FCC 2d 366 (1977).

21. *American Security Council Educational Foundation v. FCC*, *supra.*, fn. 19 at 452-453.

22. *The Christopher S. Riley Co.*, 53 FCC 2d 190 (1975).

23. H.R. 5585, 97th Cong., 2nd Sess. (1982). However, a report from the House Subcommittee on Telecommunications, Consumer Protection and Finance, titled "Telecommunications in Transition: The Status of Competition in the Telecommunications Industry," does not recommend changes in the Fairness Doctrine at this time, and it is doubtful that the bill will receive any further action. Modifications of the Fairness Doctrine were unsuccessfully proposed in H.R. 4781, 97th Cong., 1st Sess. (1981).

24. *FCC News*, Report No. 5068, "FCC Sets Forth Proposals for Amending Communications Act," Sept. 17, 1981.

25. 47 C.F.R. ss.73.1910, 73.1920, 73.1930 (1980).

26. *John B. Walsh*, 31 FCC 2d 726 (1971); see also, *New Primer on Political Broadcasting and Cablecasting*, 69 FCC 2d 2209 (1978) at 2299.

27. *Mrs. Frank Diesz*, 27 FCC 2d 859 (1971).

28. *Port Jervis Broadcasting Co.*, 56 FCC 2d 1050 (1975).

29. *Donald J. Gillard*, 39 RR 2d 1093 (1977).

30. *Howard Lockwood*, 39 RR 2d 1501 (1977).

31. *Adrian Weiss*, 58 FCC 2d 342 (1976), *review denied*, 58 FCC 2d 1389 (1976); *Walt Disney Productions, Inc.*, 33 FCC 2d 297 (1972), *aff'd.* 33 FCC 2d 835 (1972), *aff'd. sub nom.*; *Paulsen v. FCC*, 491 F.2d 887 (9th Cir. 1974).

32. Such a right of access does not violate the First Amendment by unduly circumscribing broadcasters' editorial discretion. CBS, Inc. v. FCC, 453 U.S. 367 (1981).

33. See generally, The Law of Political Broadcasting and Cablecasting, 43 Fed. Reg. 36341 (Aug. 16, 1978).

34. 47 C.F.R. ss.73.1910, 73.1920, 73.1930 (1980).

35. Public Media Center, supra., fn. 10.

36. First National Bank of Boston v. Bellotti, 435 U.S. 765 (1978).

37. Id. at 777.

38. Public Media Center, supra., fn. 10.

39. Mrs. J.R. Paul, 26 FCC 2d 591 (1969) at 592.

40. Hunger in America, 20 FCC 2d 143 (1969) at 151.

41. The Black Producers Assoc., 70 FCC 2d 1920 (1979).

42. Walton Broadcasting, Inc., 78 FCC 2d 857 (1980).

43. In nine states (Alabama, Alaska, California, Florida, Hawaii, New Hampshire, Oklahoma, South Carolina and Vermont) one insurer charges the media double premiums for libel insurance because they tend to fare poorly in libel suits in these states.

44. Sims v. KIRO, Inc., 20 Wn. App. 229 (1978), review denied, 91 Wn. 2d 1007 (1978), cert. denied, 441 U.S. 945 (1979).

45. Michigan United Conservation Clubs v. CBS News, 485 F. Supp. 893 (W.D. Mich. 1980).

46. Mansour v. Fanning, 6 Med. L. Rptr. 2055 (N.D. Cal. 1980).

47. Bravo Realty v. CBS, 6 Med L. Rptr. 1394 (Ill. App. 1980).

48. Simonson v. UPI, 500 F. Supp. 1261 (E.D. Wis. 1980). See also, Rinaldi v. Holt, Rhinehart & Winston, Inc., 386 N.Y. Supp. 2d 818 (N.Y. App. 1976).

49. Memphis Publishing Co. v. Nichols, 569 S.W.2d 412 (Tenn. Sup. Ct. 1978). However, note that in Mihalik v. Duprey, 7 Med. L. Rptr. 1258 (Mass. App. 1981), the court held just the opposite; statements in a newsletter which are insinuating and defamatory in the aggregate were ruled not to be a cause of action for libel because each individual statement was true.

50. Street v. NBC, 7 Med. L. Rptr. 1001 (6th Cir. 1981); Springer v. Viking Press, 7 Med. L. Rptr. 2040 (N.Y. Sup. Ct. 1981).

51. See Gertz v. Robert Welch, Inc. 418 U.S. 323 (1974); Hotchner v. Castillo-Puche, 551 F.2d 910 (2nd Cir. 1977), cert. denied sub nom.; Hotchner v. Doubleday & Co., Inc. 434 U.S. 834 (1977).

52. Orr v. Argus-Press Co., 586 F.2d 1108 (6th Cir. 1978), cert. denied, 440 U.S. 960 (1979).

53. Anton v. St. Louis Suburban Newspapers, Inc., 598 S.W.2d 493 (Mo. App. 1980). See also, National Association of Government Employees v. Central Broadcasting Corp., 396 N.E.2d 996 (Mass. Sup. Ct. 1979), cert. denied, 48 U.S.L.W. 3730 (May 12, 1980).

54. Good Government Group of Seal Beach v. Superior Court of Los Angeles County, 586 P.2d 572 (Cal. Sup. Ct. 1978), cert. denied, 47 U.S.L.W. 3761 (May 21, 1979); Stern v. Giovannoni, 7 Med. L. Rptr. 2135 (4th Cir. 1981), similarly holds that a jury must decide about the use of the word "swindler."

55. Bianco v. Palm Beach Newspapers, 6 Med. L. Rptr. 1484 (D. Fla. App. 1980). See also Catalano v. Pechous, 6 Med. L. Rptr. 2511 (Ill. Sup. Ct. 1980).

56. Pierce v. Capital Cities Communications, 3 Med. L. Rptr. 2259 (3rd Cir. 1978). See also Early v. Palm Beach Newspapers, Inc., 334 So.2d 50 (Fla. App. 1976), cert. denied, 439 U.S. 910 (1978); and Myers v. Boston Magazine, 6 Med. L. Rptr. 1241 (Mass. Sup. Ct. 1980).

57. Okun and Harris v. Superior Court, 29 Ca.3d 442 (Cal. Sup. Ct. 1981).

58. Rand v. N.Y. Times Co., 6 Med. L. Rptr. 1692 (N.Y. Sup. Ct. App. Div. 1980) and Pease v. Telegraph Publishing Co., 7 Med. L. Rptr. 1114 (N.H. Sup. Ct. 1981).

59. New York Times v. Sullivan, 376 U.S. 254 (1964).

60. Curtis Publishing Co. v. Butts, 388 U.S. 130 (1967).

61. Rosenbloom v. Metromedia, Inc., 403 U.S. 29 (1971).

62. Gertz v. Robert Welch, Inc., supra., fn. 51.

63. The status of a corporation as a private individual is discussed infra.

64. Arizona - Peagler v. Phoenix Newspapers, Inc., 560 P.2d 1216 (Ariz. Sup. Ct. 1977); California - Weidener v. Pacific Gas & Electric Corp., 75 Cal. App. 3d 415, 142 Cal. Rptr. 304 (Cal. App. 1977), cert. denied, 436 U.S. 918 (1978); District of Columbia - Phillips v. Evening Star Newspaper Co., 424 A.2d 78 (D.C. App. 1980); Florida (implied) - Firestone v. Time, Inc., 332 So.2d 68 (Fla. Sup. Ct. 1976); Hawaii - Cahill v. Hawaiian Paradise Park Corp., 56 Haw. 522, 543 P.2d 1356 (Haw. Sup. Ct. 1975); Illinois - Troman v. Wood, 62 Ill. 2d 184, 340 N.E.2d 292 (Ill. Sup. Ct. 1976); Kansas - Gobin v. Globe Publishing Co., 216 Kan. 223, 531 P.2d 76 (Kan. Sup. Ct. 1975); Kentucky - E.W. Scripps Co. v. Cholomondelay, 569 S.W.2d 700 (Ky. App. 1978); Maryland - General Motors Corp. v. Piskor, 277 Md. 165, 352 A.2d 810 (Md. App. 1976); Jacron Sales Co. v. Sindorf, 276 Md. 580, 350 A.2d 688 (Md. App. 1976); Massachusetts - Stone v. Essex County Newspapers, Inc., 367 Mass. 849, 330 N.E.2d 161 (Mass. Sup. Ct. 1975); Ohio - Thomas H. Maloney & Sons, Inc. v. E.W. Scripps Co., 43 Ohio App. 2d 105, 334 N.E.2d 494 (Ohio App. 1974), cert. denied, 423 U.S. 883 (1975); Oklahoma - Martin v. Griffin Television, Inc., 549 P.2d 85 (Okla. Sup. Ct. 1976); Tennessee -Memphis Publishing Co. v. Nichols, 569 S.W.2d 412 (Tenn. Sup. Ct. 1978); Texas - Foster v. Laredo Newspapers, Inc., 541 S.W.2d 809 (Texas Sup. Ct. 1976); Utah - Seegmiller v. KSL, 626 P.2d 968 (Utah Sup. Ct. 1981); Virginia - Mills v. Kingsport Times-News, 475 F. Supp. 1005 (W.D. Va. 1979); Washington - Taskett v. King Broadcasting Co., 86 Wash. 2d 439, 546 P.2d 81 (Wash. Sup. Ct. 1976).

65. Chapadeau v. Utica Observer-Dispatch, Inc., 38 N.Y. 2d 196, 379 N.Y. Sup. 61, 341 N.E.2d 569 (N.Y. App. 1975).

66. Alabama - Browing v. Birmingham News Co., 348 So.2d 455 (Ala. Sup. Ct. 1977); Connecticut - Corbett v. Register Publishing Co., 356 A.2d 472 (Conn. Sup. Ct. 1975); Georgia (negligence standard implied) - Retail Credit Co. v. Russell, 218 S.E.2d 54 (Ga. Sup. Ct. 1975); Rosanova v. Playboy Enterprises, Inc., 411 F. Supp. 440 (S.D. Ga. 1976), aff'd, 580 F.2d 859 (5th Cir. 1978); Iowa - McCarney v. Des Moines Register & Tribune Co., 239 N.W.2d 152 (Iowa Sup. Ct. 1976); Louisiana - Mashburn v. Collin, 341 So.2d 1236 (La. App. 1976), rev'd. on other grounds, 355 So.2d 879 (1977).

67. 443 U.S. 157 (1979).

68. Ibid. at 168.

69. Ibid. at 167.

70. 443 U.S. 111 (1979).

71. Brewer v. Memphis Publishing, 626 F.2d 1238 (5th Cir. 1980), cert. denied, 49 U.S.L.W. 3954 (1981); Dupler v. Mansfield Journal, 413 N.E.2d 1187 (Ohio Sup. Ct. 1980), cert. denied, 49 U.S.L.W. 3954 (1981).

72. Martin Marietta Corp. v. Evening Star Newspaper Co., 417 F. Supp. 947 (D.D.C. 1976).

73. Trans World Accounts, Inc. v. Associated Press, 425 F. Supp. 814 (N.D. Cal. 1977).

74. Reliance Insurance Co. v. Barron's, 442 F. Supp. 1341 (S.D. N.Y. 1977).

75. Friends of Animals, Inc. v. Associated Fur Manufacturers, Inc., 61 A.D.2d 141, 401 N.Y. Supp. 2d 78 (N.Y. App. 1978).

76. Steaks Unlimited v. Deaner, 6 Med. L. Rptr. 1129 (3rd Cir. 1980). See also, Bose Corp. v. Consumer's Union, 508 F. Supp. 1249 (D.Mass. 1981); and Greer v. Columbus Monthly, 7 Med. L. Rptr. 2094 (Ohio Com. Pl. 1981).

77. Economy Carpets v. Better Business Bureau, 361 So.2d 234 (La. App. 1978), cert. denied, 440 U.S. 915 (1979).

78. Peagler v. Phoenix Newspaper, Inc., supra., fn. 64.

79. Lake Havasu Estates, Inc. v. Reader's Digest, 441 F. Supp. 489 (S.D. N.Y. 1977). See also, Thomas H. Maloney & Sons, Inc. v. E.W. Scripps Co., supra. fn. 64; and Aafco Heating and Air Conditioning Co. v. Northwest Publications, Inc., 321 N.E.2d 580 (Ind. App. 1974), cert. denied, 424 U.S. 913 (1976).

80. Vegod Corp. v. American Broadcasting Companies, Inc., 25 Cal. 3d 763, 160 Cal. Rptr. 97, 603 P.2d 14 (Cal. Sup. Ct. 1979).

81. Bruno & Stillman, Inc. v. Globe Newspaper Co., 633 F.2d 583 (1st Cir. 1980).

82. Bose Corp. v. Consumer's Union, supra., fn. 76.

83. Bruno & Stillman v. Globe Newspaper Co., supra., fn. 81.

84. Gertz v. Robert Welch, Inc., supra., fn. 51; Bose Corp. v. Consumer's Union, supra., fn. 76.

85. See, Martin Marietta, supra. fn. 72; Reliance Insurance Co., supra. fn. 74; and Trans World Accounts, Inc., supra., fn. 73.

86. Arctic v. Loudoun Times Mirror, 6 Med. L. Rptr. 1433 (4th Cir. 1980), cert. denied, 449 U.S. 1102 (1981).

87. Vegod Corp. v. ABC, supra., fn. 80.

88. Rancho La Costa v. Superior Court, 6 Med. L. Rptr. 1351 (Cal. App. 1980).

89. New York Times v. Sullivan, supra., fn. 59, at 279-280.

90. Garrison v. Louisiana, 379 U.S. 64 (1964) at 74.

91. Curtis Publishing Co. v. Butts, supra., fn. 60 at 155, 158.

92. St. Amant v. Thompson, 390 U.S. 727 (1968) at 731.

93. Greenbelt Cooperative Publishing Association v. Bresler, 398 U.S. 6 (1970) at 10-11; Letter Carriers v. Austin, 418 U.S. 264 (1974) at 281.

94. Airlie Foundation, Inc. v. Evening Star Newspaper Co., 337 F. Supp. 421 (D.D.C. 1972) at 427-428.

95. Alioto v. Cowles Communications, Inc., 430 F. Supp. 1363 (N.D. Cal. 1977) at 1371, aff'd., 623 F.2d 616 (9th Cir. 1980), cert. denied, 449 U.S. 1102 (1981).

96. Holter v. WCLY, 366 So.2d 445 (Fla. App. 1978).

97. Cape Publications, Inc. v. Adams, 336 So.2d 1197 (D.Fla. App. 1976).

98. Altus Newspapers, Inc. v. Akins, 609 P.2d 1263 (Okla. Sup. Ct. 1980), cert. denied, 449 U.S. 1010 (1980).

99. Advertiser Co. v. Fulton, 388 So.2d 533 (Ala. Sup. Ct. 1980), cert. denied, 449 U.S. 1131 (1981).

100. Alioto v. Cowles Communications, Inc., supra., fn. 95.

101. Gleichenhaus v. Carlyle, No. 49, 529 (Kan., July 14, 1979).

102. DiLorenzo v. New York News, 7 Med. L. Rptr. 1452 (N.Y. App. 1981).

103. Herbert v. Lando, 441 U.S. 153 (1979).

104. Weidener v. Pacific Gas & Electric Co., supra., fn. 64.

105. In recent years, the media have begun to fight back at baseless legal actions with countersuits seeking reimbursement for attorneys' fees and defense costs, as well as damages for violations of civil rights and abuse of the judicial process. The corporation that seeks legal redress for a legitimate complaint should have nothing to fear, but a "bad faith" libel suit intended to silence or discredit the press could inspire a counter-claim. Nemeroff v. Abelson, 620 F.2d 339 (2nd Cir. 1980), rev'd. in part, 469 F. Supp. 630 (S.D. N.Y. 1979); Church of Scientology v. Siegelman, 475 F. Supp. 950 (S.D. N.Y. 1979). See also "Press Bites Back at Libel Suits," The News Media and the Law, June/July 1981, pp. 22-25 (published by The Reporters Committee for Freedom of the Press).

106. Edwards v. National Audubon Society, 556 F.2d 113 (2nd Cir. 1977), cert. denied sub nom.; Edwards v. New York Times Co., 434 U.S. 1002 (1977); contra., Dickey v. CBS, Inc., 583 F.2d 1221 (3rd Cir. 1978).

107. Edwards v. National Audubon Society, supra., fn. 106 at 120.

108. See Gertz v. Robert Welch, Inc., supra., fn. 51.

109. See, e.g., Taskett v. King Broadcasting Co., supra., fn. 64, where the director of an advertising agency who was incorrectly charged with having absconded with a client's money was held a private figure. Another example is Denny v. Mertz, 7 Med. L. Rptr. 1261 (Wis. App. 1981), in which a corporation's internal disputes were determined not to constitute a "public controversy," thus allowing the corporation's former general counsel to qualify as a private figure for a libel action against a magazine publisher.

110. Dixson v. Newsweek, Inc. 562 F.2d 626 (10th Cir. 1977).

111. Lawlor v. Gallagher Presidents' Report, Inc., 394 F. Supp. 721 (S.D. N.Y. 1975), remanded, 538 F.2d 311 (2nd Cir. 1976).

112. Waldbaum v. Fairchild Publications, Inc., 627 F.2d 1287 (D.D.C. 1980), cert. denied, 449 U.S. 898 (1980).

113. Bortell v. Citizens for Better Care, 6 Med. L. Rptr. 1797 (Mich. App. 1980).

114. Hill V. Allan, 66 Cal. Rptr. 676 (Cal. App. 1968).

115. Fowler v. Curtis Publishing Co., 182 F.2d 377 (D.C. Cir. 1950).

116. Golden Palace, Inc. v. National Broadcasting Co., 386 F. Supp. 107 (D.C. Cir. 1974), aff'd., 530 F.2d 1094 (D.D.C. 1976).

117. Dale System, Inc. v. General Teleradio, Inc., 105 F. Supp. 745 (S.D. N.Y. 1952).

118. Cal. Civ. Code Ann. s.48a(1) (1982); see, Alioto v. Cowles Communications, Inc., supra., fn. 95.

119. Code of Virginia, Title 8.01, ss.8.01-48 (1977).

120. See, for example, Fla. Stat. Ann., Title 43, ss.770.01-02 (1981); Ga. Code Ann., Title 51, s.51-5-11 (1982).

121. Ibid.; see also, Holden v. Pioneer Broadcasting Co., 365 P.2d 845 (Ore. Sup. Ct. 1961), app. dismissed and cert. denied, 370 U.S. 157 (1961).

122. See, for example, Alioto v. Cowles Communications, Inc., supra., fn. 95, where the court held that magazines were not within the purview of Cal. Civ. Code s.48a(1), and therefore no retraction demand was necessary.

123. See, Di Giorgio Corp. v. Valley Labor Citizen, 67 Cal. Rptr. 82 (Cal. App. 1968), which held that a statute restricting recovery for a defamatory statement published in a newspaper was held to protect a newspaper reporter, even as to his article's publication in another newspaper; see, also, White v. Valenta, 44 Cal. Rptr. 241 (Cal. App. 1965), where an intruder in a live television broadcast was not protected by the same statute.

124. Oasis Nite Club, Inc. v. Diebold, Inc., 261 F. Supp. 173 (D.Md. 1966); Shubert v. Columbia Pictures Corp., 189 Misc. 734, 72 N.Y. Supp. 2d 851 (N.Y. Sup. Ct. 1947), aff'd. without opinion, 80 N.Y. Supp. 2d 724 (N.Y. App. 1948).

125. United States v. Morton Salt Co., 388 U.S. 632 (1950).

126. Dolin, S.L., "Shield Laws: The Legislative Response to Journalistic Privilege," 26 Cleve. St. L. Rev. 453 (1977).

127. Nelson, H., "The Newsman's Privilege Against Disclosure of Confidential Sources and Information," 24 Vand. L. Rev. 667 (1971).

128. Ibid.

129. People ex rel. Mooney v. Sheriff, 269 N.Y. 291, 199 N.E. 415 (N.Y. App. 1936).

130. State v. Sandstrom, 224 Kan. 573, 581 P.2d 812 (Kan. Sup. Ct. 1978), cert. denied sub nom.; Pennington v. Kansas, 440 U.S. 929 (1979).

131. Garland v. Torre, 259 F.2d 545 (2nd Cir. 1958), cert. denied, 358 U.S. 910 (1958).

132. Branzburg v. Hayes, 408 U.S. 665 (1972).

133. See, e.g., United States v. Pretzinger, 542 F.2d 517 (9th Cir. 1976) at 520; United States v. Liddy, 478 F.2d 586 (D.C. Cir. 1972) at 587; United States v. Orsini, 424 F. Supp. 229 (E.D. N.Y. 1976) at 232, aff'd., 559 F.2d 1206 (2nd Cir. 1977), cert. denied, 434 U.S. 997 (1977); Zalenka v. State, 83 Wis. 2d 601, 266 N.W.2d 279 (Wis. Sup. Ct. 1978); State v. Sandstrom, supra., fn. 130; Florida v. Hurston, 3 Med. L. Rptr. 2295 (Fla. Cir. 1978); State v. St. Peter, 315 A.2d 254 (Vt. Sup. Ct. 1974); Richmond Newspapers, Inc. v. Virginia, 448 U.S. 555 (1980).

134. See, e.g., Carey v. Hume, 492 F.2d 631 (D.C. Cir. 1974), cert. denied, 417 U.S. 938 (1974); Baker v. F&F Investment, 470 F.2d 778 (2nd Cir. 1972), cert. denied, 411 U.S. 966 (1973); Citicorp v. Interbank Card Ass'n, 478 F. Supp. 756 (S.D. N.Y. 1978).

135. In Re Farber, 78 N.J. 259, 394 A.2d 330 (N.J. Sup. Ct. 1978), cert. denied, 439 U.S. 997 (1978); Miller v. Transamerican Press, Inc., 621 F.2d 721 (5th Cir. 1980), cert. denied, 450 U.S. 1041 (1981).

136. New York Times Co. v. Jascalevich, 439 U.S. 1301 (1978).

137. In Re Powers, 4 Med. L. Rptr. 1600 (D.Vt. 1978); Michigan v. Smith, 4 Med. L. Rptr. 1753 (Mich. Cir. 1978). In Powers, the court stated that an earlier Vermont decision, recognizing a qualified privilege, could no longer be considered the law in view of Justice White's statement in Farber. See also, U.S. v. Cuthbertson, 630 F.2d 139 (3rd Cir. 1980), where CBS was ordered to reveal sources and information relevant to the trial of a food franchise on charges of conspiracy and fraud.

138. CBS v. Superior Ct., 149 Cal. Rptr. 421 (Cal. App. 1978); U.S. v. Hubbard, 493 F. Supp. 202 (D.C. Cir. 1979).

139. In Re Farber, supra., fn. 135; Pennington v. Kansas, supra., fn. 130.

140. Gulliver's Periodicals, Ltd. v. Chas. Levy Circulating Co., 455 F. Supp. 1197 (N.D. Ill. 1978); Hart v. Playboy Enterprises, 4 Med. L. Rptr. 1616 (D.Kan. 1978); Rancho La Costa v. Penthouse, supra., fn. 88; Amato v. Fellner, 4 Med. L. Rptr. 1552 (Wis. Cir. 1978).

141. Baker v. F&F Investment, supra., fn. 134; Riley v. City of Chester, 612 F.2d 708 (3rd Cir. 1979); Miller v. Transamerican Press, Inc., supra., fn. 135; Cervantes v. Time, Inc., 464 F.2d 986 (8th Cir. 1972); Silkwood v. Kerr-McGee Corp., 563 F.2d 433 (10th Cir. 1977).

142. Herbert v. Lando, supra., fn. 103. See also, Greenleigh Associates v. New York Post, 6 Med. L. Rptr. 2423 (N.Y. App. 1980) and Resorts International v. New Jersey Monthly, 7 Med. L. Rptr. 2025 (N.J. Super. 1981), examples of cases in which state courts ordered disclosure of

142. Contd...
editorial processes. Similarly, in Gagnon v. Fremont District Ct., 7 Med. L. Rptr. 1755 (Colo. Sup. Ct. 1981), the state court forced disclosure of unpublished material relevant to the libel suit.

143. Avilla v. Shirai, Civ. No. 56035 (Hawaii Cir. Ct., Honolulu County, Sept. 12, 1979); see also, Miller v. Transamerican Press, supra., fn. 135.

144. Brown v. Traub, cert. denied, 444 U.S. 979 (1979).

145. Corsetti v. Commonwealth, No. 80-724 (Mass. Super. Ct., Middlesex County, March 20, 1980), on appeal, No. 2148.

146. Downing v. Monitor Publishing Co., 6 Med. L. Rptr. 1193 (N.H. Sup. Ct. 1980) (which resulted in an out-of-court settlement); DeRoburt v. Gannett, 6 Med. L. Rptr. 2473 (D. Haw. 1981).

147. "A Study in Governmental Separation of Powers: Judicial Response to State Shield Laws," 66 Geo. L. J. 1273 (1978) (hereinafter "Shield Law Study").

148. Ibid.

149. Congress has attempted to enact a Federal Shield Law but has met with little success. The year after Branzburg, supra., fn. 132, more than 60 bills were introduced, with just one being reported out of subcommittee -- only to die at the committee level.

150. Los Angeles Memorial Colosseum Comm. v. NFL, No. 78-3523 (C.D. Cal. Jan. 5, 1981); Howland v. Justice Court, No. 7549 (Cal. Super. Ct., Trinity County, filed Feb. 2, 1981). See

150. Contd...
also, Miller v. Transamerican Press, supra., fn. 135, in which the California shield law and a Texas shield law were deemed by a U.S. Court of Appeals to be no protection for the confidentiality of a source in a libel case.

151. See, e.g., In Re Farber, supra., fn. 135; Michigan v. Smith, supra., fn. 137; In Re Investigative File, 4 Med. L. Rptr. 1865 (D.Mont. 1978).

152. Pavlak v. Searle, No. 435-444 (Minn. Dist. Ct., Ramsey County, Jan. 2, 1979).

153. Steaks Unlimited v. Deaner, supra., fn. 76.

154. Mazzella v. Philadelphia Newspapers, Inc., 479 F. Supp. 523 (E.D. N.Y. 1979).

155. Galella v. Onasis, 487 F.2d 986 (2nd Cir. 1973).

156. Dietemann v. Time, Inc., 449 F.2d 245 (9th Cir. 1971).

157. Florida Publishing Co. v. Fletcher, 340 So.2d 914 (Fla. Sup. Ct. 1976), cert. denied, 431 U.S. 930 (1976).

158. Le Mistral, Inc. v. CBS, 402 N.Y. Supp. 2d 815 (N.Y. App. 1978).

159. Gertz v. Robert Welch, Inc., supra., fn. 51.

160. Ibid.

161. Ibid.; Davis v. Schuchat, 510 F.2d 731 (D.C. Cir. 1975).

162. Maheu v. Hughes Tool Co., 569 F.2d 459 (9th Cir. 1978).

163. *Sierra Life Insurance v. Magic Valley Newspapers*, 4 Med. L. Rptr. 1689 (D.Idaho 1978).

164. *Pring v. Penthouse International*, 7 Med. L. Rptr. 1101 (D.Wyo. 1981). (Award was later reduced).

165. *Burnett v. National Enquirer*, 7 Med. L. Rptr. 1321 (Cal. Super. 1981). (Award was later reduced to $800,000).

166. Statistics from Fairness/Political Broadcasting Branch, Complaints and Compliance Division, Broadcast Bureau, Federal Communications Commission, 1919 M Street, N.W., Washington, D.C. 20554.

167. Franklin, Marc A., "Suing Media for Libel: A Litigation Study" (1981) *American Bar Foundation Research Journal* 795. See also, Franklin, "Winners and Losers and Why: A Study of Defamation Litigation" (1980) *American Bar Foundation Research Journal* 457, an earlier study which compares media libel cases to non-media ones.

168. *Ibid.*

169. The "innocent construction rule" calls for the dismissal of all cases in which the challenged language is susceptible to a reasonably non-defamatory interpretation, no matter what meaning was intended by the defendant or understood by the audience.

170. This information, cited in the 1981 Franklin study, is being developed for publication by Professor Jerome Skelnick, School of Law, University of California at Berkeley, and Eliot Cahn, Manager of the Litigation Support Program at SRI International, Menlo Park, California.

171. Franklin, "Suing Media for Libel: A Litigation Study," *supra.*, fn. 167 at 829.

172. Study by Prof. Dennis Hale, Bowling Green State University, reported in "First Amendment Congress Newsletter" (Washington, D.C.: The Newspaper Center), August 1981.

APPENDIX A
SUMMARY OF 1981 FAIRNESS RULINGS

WTAX - Concerned Taxpayers of Illinois' 21st Congressional District - Letter or Admonition issued where station broadcast sponsorship identification of announcements as "Concerned Taxpayers of Illinois' 21st Congressional District." Such identification does not inform public by whom it is being persuaded.

January 2, 1981

KVIP - Mr. Frank Treadway - Merely because a subject has received media coverage does not demonstrate that the issue is controversial or of public importance.

January 15, 1981

WMAZ & WMAZ-TV - John S. Warchak, Esq. - A Fairness Doctrine complaint re: both stations broadcasting alleged pro-black programming and not giving white equal time.

January 15, 1981

WBPZ-AM-FM - Mr. George Miller - Where a complainant alleges a personal attack, or a Fairness Doctrine violation occurred during the broadcast of an editorial, it is within the licensee's discretion, not the complainant's, to determine the amount of time the complainant should receive to respond, provided that the licensee acts reasonably and absent bad faith. A reference to a caller of a talk show program as the "cousin" of the complainant is not sufficient to demonstrate a personal attack occurred.

February 23, 1981

WFAA-TV - James Robison Evangelistic Association - Application for Review DENIED. Applicant failed to demonstrate that licensee acted unreasonably in (1) determining that Applicant's discussion of homosexuality constituted discussion of a controversial issue of public importance; (2) cancelling Applicant's religious program because he discussed homosexuality on program; and (3) establishing station policy that discussion of controversial issues of public importance be excluded from religious programming. Applicant also failed to demonstrate that the Fairness Doctrine has an unconstitutional, chilling effect on religious broadcasting. 85 FCC 2d 642

A-February 26, 1981
March 5, 1981

WBMK - Mr. Gerald Henley - A personal attack complainant must specify the words or statements made, which adversely reflect upon the individual's honesty, character, integrity or like personal characteristics. Even if a personal attack is broadcast, a licensee is not required to provide the individual with notification and an opportunity to respond, where the individual is present and able to respond.

March 6, 1981

WOWT(TV) - Mr. Don R. Cunningham - Even though a complainant complies with a station's procedures for responding to editorials, the licensee does not violate the Fairness Doctrine by not accepting the complainant's response. The licensee's responsibility under the Fairness Doctrine is only to present both sides of the issue.

March 9, 1981

KSTP-TV - Minnesota Farmers Union - Complainant failed to demonstrate that the use or alleged misuse of the Union's educational funds was the subject of vigorous debate among substantial elements of the community, or that the issue would likely have a substantial impact upon a significant number of the community.

A-March 31, 1981
March 31, 1981

KCOS-TV - Mr. Oscar B. White - There was no evidence that the station was "actively involved" in the production and staging of a news documentary.

Even if there was active involvement, the facts would not amount to "significant" staging of a news event. In addition, this ruling contained a discussion of sponsorship identification.

April 10, 1981

CBS - Mr. Ed Armstrong - Complainant failed to establish that licensee acted unreasonably where, assuming that the issue of motorcycle helmet wearing is a controversial issue of public importance, licensee presented 30 seconds supporting wearing of helmets, and 15 seconds against the issue in a programming segment of 10-12 minutes. Complainant provided no information on overall programming regarding the issue.

April 13, 1981

WJFD(FM) - Mr. Jose Pedro Bio - No Commission action is warranted where the complainant is not the candidate, or a person with knowledge of all the facts, including information obtained by the candidate. No Commission action is warranted on a personal attack complaint where the complainant fails to show the personal attack occurred during the discussion of a controversial issue of public importance, and where the station's offer to the complainant of time to respond is still outstanding.

April 14, 1981

KERO-TV, KJEO, KMST, KRCR-TV, KRON-TV & KTXL - Environmental Defense Fund, etc. - Complainants failed to satisfy their burden of proof in two material respects. They neither showed that the issue was controversial, nor did they demonstrate any basis for the claim that licensees' overall programming was imbalanced.

A-April 17, 1981
April 17, 1981

WFPL(FM) - Mr. & Mrs. Robert L. Miller - Application for Review of Broadcast Bureau's June 26, 1980 ruling is DENIED. The Bureau ruled that commentary criticizing "right to lifers" does not name an identifiable group and does not entitle any specific "right to life" group to redress. 86 FCC 2d 138

A-April 9, 1981
April 17, 1981

WRC - Mr. Paul A. LaFranchise - Where a station has offered a complainant opportunity to review program logs for a weekend in question, four or five hours of time to review tapes of the weekend, or the opportunity to listen to the entire 36 hours in question, if complainant will pay for union engineer; it appears that the station has complied with Section 73.1850 of the Commission's Rules.

May 6, 1981

WNAC-TV - Dr. Richard Wilson - Complainant failed to show that licensee was unreasonable in broadcasting 25 spot announcements (18 minutes) supporting use of nuclear energy as opposed to one-hour program against use of nuclear energy. Complainant also failed to demonstrate that licensee was unreasonable in not choosing group that complainant represented to present contrasting viewpoint on the issue.

May 28, 1981

KERO-TV - Ms. Sheila Wyllie - Station admonished for apparent violations of Section 73.1212, in that station broadcast program containing discussion of controversial issue of public importance without proper sponsorship identification, and did not place list of officers of sponsoring corporation in public file at time of broadcast.

June 3, 1981

WBZ-TV - Mr. Leo J. Coveney - Complainant failed to establish that alleged personal attack occurred during discussion of controversial issue of public importance. He also failed to show that the person allegedly attacked was not offered reasonable opportunity to respond. In addition, complainant failed to provide extrinsic evidence of alleged false information broadcast.

June 10, 1981

WLBT-TV - Richard Barrett, Esq. - Application for Review of Broadcast Bureau ruling of December 10, 1980 IS DENIED.

A-June 30, 1981
July 7, 1981

Paul Loveday, Esq. - Californians for Smoking and No Smoking Sections - Where a complainant alleges that a third party is the actual sponsor of advertisements and should be designated as such in the tag-line. The complainant must show that the third party: (1) actually paid for the advertising time; and (2) exercised editorial control over the advertisements. 87 FCC 2d 492

A-July 30, 1981
August 7, 1981

WTMJ-AM-TV & WTKI-FM - Mayor Henry W. Maier - Complainant failed to provide extrinsic evidence that the licensee intentionally misstated and suppressed facts in its station editorials. He failed to establish that the editorials discussed controversial issues or that the station did not provide reasonable opportunity for the discussion of contrasting viewpoints. Further, complainants did not establish that the editorials contained attacks upon his honesty, character, integrity or like personal qualities during the discussion of controversial issues of public importance.

August 18, 1981

KBFL(FM) - Mr. Wayne Lemons - Petition for Reconsideration of Broadcast Bureau's November 26, 1980 ruling, as it pertains to the Fairness Doctrine complaints, IS DENIED. With respect to the allegation of station editorializing in violation of Section 399(a) of the Communications Act of 1934, as amended, it will be held IN OBEYANCE.

A-August 18, 1981
August 19, 1981

KVIP - Mr. Frank Treadway - A fairness complainant bears the burden of defining the issue and explaining why it is controversial and of public importance.

August 19, 1981

WBPZ-AM-FM - George Miller - Miller's Application for Review was DENIED. The licensee was not unreasonable in determining that Miller was not personally attacked in an editorial, in a talk show program or in a newscast. Further, the licensee's decision to limit its response to the editorial to two-three minutes was within its discretion and was reasonable under the Fairness Doctrine.

A-September 22, 1981
September 25, 1981

WOWT(TV) - Mr. Don R. Cunningham - Application for Review of Broadcast Bureau's March 9, 1981 ruling is DENIED.

A-September 22, 1981
September 25, 1981

KCOS-TV - Oscar B. White - The Commission held that the incidental appearances of county employees dressed as prisoners in a documentary concerning a jail bond issue did not amount to news staging. The Commission stated that the Fairness Doctrine does not require a licensee to "equalize" the presentation of contrasting views. Finally, the Commission admonished the licensee for failure to comply with the sponsorship identification requirements. 87 FCC 2d 954

A-September 22, 1981
September 29, 1981

WFBA - Mr. Eulogio Cardona y Beltran - A personal attack complainant must establish that a controversial issue of public importance was discussed and that a personal attack was directed to him.

November 9, 1981

J. Curtis Harge, Esq. (NCPAC) - With the exception of "reasonable access" for federal candidates and "equal opportunities" for political candidates generally, the Supreme Court has affirmed Commission determination that "public interest" standard, which incorporates First Amendment principles, does not require private right of access. Fairness Doctrine is applicable to any announcement accepted by broadcaster which contains discussion of a controversial issue of public importance, and free time may be required under the Cullman Doctrine outside compaign periods. 88 FCC 2d 626

November 20, 1981

WBZ-TV - Mr. Leo J. Coveney - Application for Review of Broadcast Bureau's June 10, 1981 ruling IS DENIED.

A-November 12, 1981
November 24, 1981

WVMG - Mrs. James Scott Horne - Licensee may discuss or editorialize on matters in which it has personal nonbroadcast interest, as long as it reveals to its audience the extent and nature of its interest. When licensee's interest is clear on the face of subject programming, express disclosure not required. Solicitation of funds in broadcast is not prohibited, as long as funds are utilized for stated purpose.

November 27, 1981

CBS - Alan P. Dye, Esq. - Complainant must furnish Commission with prima facie Fairness Doctrine complaint. Complainant failed to identify the issue with sufficient specificity, and failed to satisfactorily assert that broadcaster did not present contrasting viewpoints in its overall programming.

December 10, 1981

J. Curtis Harge, Esq. (NCPAC) - With the exception of "reasonable access" for federal candidates and "equal opportunities" for political candidates generally, the Supreme Court has affirmed Commission determination that the "public interest" standard, which incorporates First Amendment principles, does not require private right of access. Fairness Doctrine is applicable to any announcement accepted by broadcaster which contains discussion of a controversial issue of public importance.

December 18, 1981

APPENDIX B
SOURCES OF INFORMATION

The following resources may provide useful explanations and information.

(1) The actual text of the Federal Communications Commission regulations can be found in the Code of Federal Regulations, supported by the Communications Act of 1934, as amended.

(2) Friendly, Fred. The Good Guys, The Bad Guys and the First Amendment (New York: Random House, 1976).

(3) Simmons, Steven J. The Fairness Doctrine and the Media (Berkeley: University of California, 1978).

(4) The Law of Political Broadcasting and Cablecasting: A Political Primer, available from the Federal Communications Commission, 1919 M Street, N.W., Washington, D.C. 20554.

(5) Political Broadcasting Catechism, National Association of Broadcasters, c. 1980, available from Publications Manager, National Association of Broadcasters, 1771 N Street, N.W., Washington, D.C. 20036, for $9.00.

(6) The News Media and the Law, published four-five times a year by The Reporters Committee for Freedom of the Press, 1125 15th Street, N.W., Room 403, Washington, D.C. 20005.

(7) Libel Defense Resource Center, 708 3rd Avenue 32nd Floor, New York, N.Y. 10017. This organization provides information to the media to aid them in their legal defenses.

(8) "At Issue: Access to Television", published by Kaiser Aluminum and Chemical Corporation, 300 Lakeside Drive, Oakland, California 94643.

(9) Geller, Henry. The Fairness Doctrine in Broadcasting: Problems & Suggested Courses of Action. (Santa Monica, CA: The Rand Corporation, 1973). R-1412-FF.

(10) Shapiro, Andrew O. Media Access. (Boston: Little, Brown and Co., 1976).

(11) Bennett, Robert W. A Lawyers' Sourcebook: Representing the Audience in Broadcast Proceedings. (New York: Office of Communications, United Church of Christ, January 1974).

(12) Franklin, Marc A. "Winners and Losers and Why: A Study of Defamation Litigation." 1980 American Bar Foundation Research Journal, 457, and "Suing Media for Libel: A Litigation Study", 1981 American Bar Foundation Research Journal, 795.

(13) Sack, Robert D. Libel, Slander & Related Problems. (New York: Practicing Law Institute, 1980). Appendices include a listing of state statutes of limitation for defamation actions and full texts of state retraction statutes and state shield laws.

INDEX

-A-

-D-

-H-

-J-

-O-

-P-

-Y-